BANGOR OCCAS  KW-442-717

General Editor: Jack Revell

Professor of Economics,
University College of North Wales,
Bangor

NUMBER 15

THE IMF: PAST, PRESENT AND FUTURE

E. M. Ainley

UNIVERSITY OF WALES PRESS

1979

(C) UNIVERSITY OF WALES PRESS, 1979

ISBN 0 7083 0715 9

ISSN 0306-9338

Printed by photo-litho at the University College of North Wales, Bangor

EDITOR'S NOTE

The main intention of the series of Bangor Occasional Papers in Economics is to provide a vehicle for the publication of the results of research carried out in the two research institutes at Bangor, the Institute of Economic Research (specializing in regional economics, the economics of tourism and port economics) and the Institute of European Finance. The series also includes adaptations of theses and dissertations by research students in the Department of Economics and contributions by academic colleagues in other universities.

JACK REVELL

University College of North Wales
Bangor

Volumes in the Series

1. P. G. Sadler, B. H. Archer & Christine Owen, *Regional Income Multipliers*, 1973 (second impression 1974)

2. Brian Archer, *The Impact of Domestic Tourism*, 1973 (second impression 1974)

3. David W. Green, *The Canadian Financial System since 1965*, 1974

4. Jeffrey P. Owens, *The Growth of the Euro-Dollar Market*, 1974

5. Jack Revell, *Solvency and Regulation of Banks*, 1975

6. Richard de Vane, *Second Home Ownership: A Case Study*, 1975

7. Ade. T. Ojo, *The Nigerian Financial System*, 1976

8. Peter Sadler, *Regional Development in Ethiopia*, 1976

9. Brian Archer, *Demand Forecasting in Tourism*, 1976

10. Brian Archer, *Tourism in The Bahamas and Bermuda: Two Case Studies*, 1977

11. Brian Archer, *Tourism Multipliers: the State of the Art*, 1977

12. R. C. G. Varley, *Tourism in Fiji: Some Economic and Social Problems*, 1978

13. Basil Dalamagas, *A Value Added Tax for Greece*, 1978

14. Jack Revell (ed.), *Competition and Regulation of Banks*, 1978

CONTENTS

LIST OF TABLES

LIST OF ABBREVIATIONS

General

BIS — Bank for International Settlements
COMECON — Council for Mutual Economic Assistance
    (USSR, Bulgaria, Hungary, East Germany, Poland, Romania,
    Czechoslovakia, Mongolia and Cuba)
EEC — European Economic Community
    (Belgium, Denmark, France, Ireland, Italy, Luxembourg,
    Netherlands, United Kingdom and West Germany)
EMCF — European Monetary Co-operation Fund
EMUA — European monetary unit of account
EPC — Economic Policy Committee of the OECD
FDIC — Federal Deposit Insurance Corporation
    (United States)
FRB — Federal Reserve Board
    (United States)
FRBNY — Federal Reserve Bank of New York
FSF — Financial Support Facility
    (OECD - never operational)
GATT — General Agreement on Tariffs and Trade
G.10 — Group of ten major industrial countries
    (Belgium, Canada, France, Italy, Japan, Netherlands, Sweden
    United Kingdom, United States and West Germany)
IBRD — International Bank for Reconstruction and Development
    (the 'World Bank')
IDA — International Development Association
    ('soft' loan agency of World Bank group)
ICAs — International commodity agreements
IPC — Integrated Programme for Commodities
LDCs — Less developed (or 'developing') countries: broadly defined
    to exclude only OECD, OPEC and COMECON members
MSFs — Countries 'most seriously affected' by the 1973-74 oil crisis
OECD — Organisation for Economic Co-operation and Development
    (Australia, Austria, Belgium, Canada, Denmark, Finland,
    France, Greece, Iceland, Ireland, Italy, Japan, Luxembourg,
    Netherlands, New Zealand, Norway, Portugal, Spain, Sweden,
    Switzerland, Turkey, United Kingdom, United States and
    West Germany)
OPEC — Organisation of Petroleum-Exporting Countries
    (Algeria, Ecuador, Gabon, Indonesia, Iran, Iraq, Kuwait,
    Libya, Nigeria, Qatar, Saudi Arabia, United Arab Emirates,
    Venezuela)
UAE — United Arab Emirates
    (Abu Dhabi, Dubai, Sharjah, Ras-al-khimah, Umm-al-Quwain,
    Ajman and Fujeirah)
UNCTAD — United Nations Conference on Trade and Development
WP3 — Working party number 3 of the OECD Economic Policy Committee
    (Canada, France, Italy, Japan, Netherlands, Sweden,
    Switzerland, United Kingdom, United States and West Germany)

ABBREVIATIONS (Contd.) ..

International Monetary Fund

BSF   -   Buffer Stock Facility
C20   -   Committee of Twenty (1972-74)
CFF   -   Compensatory Finance Facility
EBD   -   Executive Board Decision
EFF   -   Extended Fund Facility
GAB   -   General Arrangements to Borrow
            (established by G.10 countries and Switzerland)
IFS   -   International Financial Statistics
            (published by the IMF)
SDRs -   Special drawing rights
SFF   -   Supplementary Financing Facility

Miscellaneous

FY   -   Financial year
GDP -   Gross domestic product
GNP -   Gross national product

PREFACE

Since 1972 the international economy has been disrupted by the dramatic rise in oil prices, major inflation and serious recession. Adjustment to these changes has been very uneven, not only between the principal groups of countries — industrial, primary-producing and under-developed — but within the various groups as well. In many cases unprecedented current account deficits have been financed by external borrowing on a large scale, mainly from commercial banks. This in turn has exposed the banks to considerable risks and there have been several instances of rescheduling or refinancing since 1975.

The role of the IMF in dealing with the problems has been relatively minor. Its influence has been limited by the failure of the 1972-76 reform exercise and the inadequacy of its resources compared with deficit countries' financing needs. The theoretical basis of the IMF's authority, the international monetary system established at Bretton Woods and codified in the IMF Articles of Agreement, has given way to widespread floating and a general reluctance to accept supra-national discipline. The 1978 Amended Articles, which incorporate the main recommendations of the Committee of Twenty, leave important gaps likely to restrict the IMF's future effectiveness. At the same time official credit from the IMF and other sources has not been expanded on the necessary scale. The IMF's influence has been confined to the few countries which have used its resources mainly, although not exclusively, in the form of special facilities with easy terms. Ordinary IMF finance has widely been judged not to be worth the cost (in terms of conditions) and has been used very much as a last resort.

The IMF is now at a crossroads. Prospects of a substantial medium-term improvement in the global payments imbalance are negligible, and growing concern over commercial bank exposure in individual countries and the inadequacy of non-IMF official financing initiatives make it imperative that the IMF extend its role. This could be achieved by full use of the surveillance powers in the Amended Articles, a radical overhaul of IMF resources and more flexible application of conditions, adapted to the longer-term nature of present problems. In practice these changes would be controversial and take time to implement, given the political divisions and institutional rigidities within the IMF. The future may therefore lie with closer IMF-IBRD co-operation, in the form of a new Washington institution, and with closer IMF-commercial bank links through exchanges of information and parallel loans.

This study seeks to explain the need for a stronger IMF, the ways in which the IMF could and should be strengthened and the most likely outcome of each possible initiative. Chapters One, Two and Three outline the structure and working of the IMF, the shortcomings of the 1945-71 system and the failure of the international monetary reform exercise of 1972-76. Chapters Four and Five analyse the present and prospective

developments in international adjustment to 1982 with emphasis on the
scale and distribution of current account deficits and on the part played
in financing them by the commercial banks.   Chapter Six examines the
potential influence of the IMF on members' future adjustment policies
through consultations, sanctions, exchange rate supervision and lending
conditions.   In Chapter Seven the future financing role of the IMF and
alternative means of increasing its resources are reviewed in detail;
and finally Chapter Eight considers the possibilities for a new IMF-IBRD
institution and closer IMF-commercial bank co-operation.

        The author wishes to acknowledge the considerable help and
encouragement received from colleagues in the Bank of England.   Needless
to say, the views expressed herein are the author's own and in no way
reflect those of the Bank of England.   The author would also like to
thank Glenys Harris for typing the first draft and Lilian Lund for typing
the final version.   The preliminary research was done between May and
September 1977 and the paper was completed in April 1978.   Inevitably
the study reflects the preoccupations of this period and risks being
overtaken by subsequent events.   But although the emphasis in international monetary affairs is constantly changing — for example, from
LDC debt problems in 1976 to the decline of the dollar in late 1977 —
the basic problems seem likely to persist for a considerable time in the
future.   Indeed it is because these problems are long-term ones, which
can only be solved gradually through concerted international action, that
there is an urgent need for a stronger IMF.

                                        E. M. AINLEY

June 1978

CHAPTER ONE

THE INTERNATIONAL MONETARY FUND:
ORIGINS AND STRUCTURE

The International Monetary Fund (IMF) has acted as the central organisation in international monetary and financial matters for over thirty years. The procedures which it has developed and some of the problems which it has encountered can be traced back to the original Agreement which is examined below.

Origins and aims

The existence of an international monetary 'system' stems from the IMF Articles of Agreement negotiated at Bretton Woods in 1944. This framework, amended in 1969 when the SDR scheme was introduced and, more comprehensively, in 1978, has — very broadly — governed financial relations between member countries in the post-war period.

The original Articles were a compromise between the ideas of White — then Under-Secretary at the United States Treasury — which centred around an International Stabilisation Fund and the proposal for an International Clearing Union developed by Keynes, leader of the United Kingdom delegation to Bretton Woods. Perhaps inevitably the influence of White, as representative of the stronger economic power, was predominant. His more conservative approach reflected the belief that the United States would remain a large and persistent creditor, whereas the ambitious proposals of Keynes were concerned largely with avoiding the contractionary effects on world trade and prosperity of inadequate international reserves. The different preoccupations of potential debtor and potential creditor countries have limited the extent of co-operation within the IMF to the present day.

Both the Keynes and the White plans, however, were governed by a common purpose — the avoidance of a relapse into the disorderly conditions of the 1930s. That governments were prepared to surrender what is even now a considerable degree of national sovereignty to an untried organisation was evidence of the damage caused by the pursuit of competitive exchange rate depreciation and autarchic protectionist policies. This was reflected in Article I of the 1944 Agreement which set out the aims of the IMF, namely:

(i) to promote international monetary co-operation;
(ii) to facilitate the growth of world trade (and thereby the promotion of high levels of employment and real income);

1

(iii) to promote exchange stability by maintaining orderly exchange arrangements among members and avoiding competitive depreciation; and

(iv) to establish a multilateral system of current payments and eliminate exchange restrictions.

In order that members would be able to carry out these obligations, even when in economic difficulties, the IMF would stand ready to:

(v) make its resources temporarily available to them under adequate safeguards, thus providing them with opportunity to correct maladjustments in their balance of payments without resorting to measures destructive of national or international prosperity.

The clear implication of (v) is that the Fund is not, and never has been, a development institution. It is designed to provide medium-term conditional finance to meet temporary balance of payments problems. It does not disburse long-term concessional funds for development or for basic structural adjustments, which is the function of other national and international agencies. IMF credit is of a revolving character and is available to all members, regardless of development status, which accords with the Fund's essentially monetary role.

In recent years, however, the nature of Fund operations has been substantially modified through a variety of special facilities of particular benefit to developing countries. Some creditors, such as West Germany and the United States, are now uneasy that the IMF may be developing into an aid-giving institution and this has important implications for the efforts in the late 1970s to increase the Fund's resources (as described more fully in Chapters Six and Seven).

Finance

One of the most significant differences between White and Keynes was the degree to which the new organisation should be passive in the provision of assistance. Keynes envisaged automatic access to facilities within generous quantitative limits, adjusted each year and related to the average of imports and exports over several years. White, on the other hand, thought in terms of controlled and supervised access within fairly restrictive limits.

In the event, the question of whether access to the Fund should be a right or a privilege was not settled until the early 1950s. The wording of the provisions governing the use of the Fund's resources (Original Article V, 3) was not explicit on this point and, in any case, the IMF was hardly used in the first years of operation, mainly because its role was taken over by the US programme of Marshall Aid. In 1950, for example, there were no drawings at all. In 1952 the adoption of the Rooth plan, drawn up by the then IMF Managing Director, established the IMF's right to examine and comment on the economic and financial policies of members. It also laid down the maximum term of drawings, normally three to five years. In the same year standby arrangements were introduced allowing members to draw up to a specified amount within a fixed period of time (one or two years). The requirement of close consultation during the life of the standby enabled the IMF to refuse an instalment of credit if agreed policies were not adhered to.   Since 1953 the standby has become the usual means of access to Fund resources.

The amount that countries may draw (i.e. borrow) is dependent on their quotas (subscriptions), which largely determine members' rights and obligations in the IMF.   They determine not only access but contributions to Fund credit and voting power as well.   They are decided with reference to detailed economic formulae adjusted for special factors, such as the reserve role of sterling, and by straightforward bargaining. Very broadly they reflect members' importance in the world economy.   The Fund has tried to maintain a reasonable balance between quotas of debtor and creditor countries to avoid liquidity strains.

General quota reviews are held 'at intervals of not more than five years' and changes in quotas are subject to an 85% majority vote in the Board of Governors and the consent of each member concerned.   Since 1945 there have been six such reviews and the size of the Fund has risen from SDR 8 billion in 1950 to SDR 39 billion in 1978.   Special increases or increases less than a general increase have sometimes been awarded to members whose quotas were seriously out of line with their relative economic position.

Under the Original Articles members were required to pay 25% of their quotas in gold and 75% in their own currencies.   Under the 1978 Second Amendment to the Articles (the 'Amended Articles') the 25% or 'reserve tranche' will no longer be paid in gold but in Special Drawing Rights (SDRs) or in currencies which the Fund is prepared to accept.   A member's indebtedness to the IMF starts at the point where the Fund's holdings of its currency exceed 75% of quota.   When Fund holdings rise to 100% of quota a member is said to have used its gold or reserve tranche. Thereafter a member may draw a maximum of four 'credit tranches', each of which is usually equal to 25% of quota.   In other words a member may borrow until Fund holdings of its currency are equal to 200% of quota. From January 1976 to March 1978 the limit on individual credit tranches was raised, temporarily, to 36.25% of quota making an overall limit of 245%.   These limits are waived rarely and then only in circumstances of particular need.

When a member (for example, country X) draws on the Fund, it 'purchases' the currency of other members (countries Y and Z) with its own currency.   A drawing thus results in an increase in Fund holdings of country X's currency and a corresponding decrease in its holdings of the currencies purchased (those of countries Y and Z).   Country X pays interest (charges) to the IMF when Fund holdings of its currency exceed 100% of quota and, conversely, the IMF pays interest (remuneration) to countries Y and Z when its holdings of their currencies fall below 75% of quota.   Under the Amended Articles the quota level at which remuneration is payable to creditor countries is subject to a more complex formula (Amended Article V, 9) but the principle is the same.   When country X draws it also undertakes to reverse the transaction by 're-purchasing' (buying back) its own currency, with currencies acceptable to the Fund, after three to five years.

Usable currencies, i.e. those which the Fund can lend (Y and Z in the above example) are chosen on the basis of certain broad criteria which were given formal approval by the IMF Executive Board in 1962 and which have been written into the Amended Articles, as described more fully in Chapter Seven.   These criteria take account of the balance of payments and reserve positions of countries whose currencies are considered for drawings (Y and Z), as well as the Fund's holdings of those currencies. As a result of this system of selection, which is embodied in quarterly currency budgets, most drawings tend to be made up of a number of currencies (as in the above example). There is provision for conversion of the currencies drawn (those of Y and Z) into the currency needed by the drawing country (X) for making international payments.

Prior to 1978, IMF operations and transactions were conducted through a General Account and a Special Drawing Account. The latter was established in 1969-70 to administer the SDR scheme which involved nearly all IMF members. All other business was transacted through the General Account: its resources were composed of quota subscriptions, interest charges on drawings and other payments by members; and were used for IMF lending in the credit tranches and under the compensatory finance, buffer stock and extended fund facilities. These resources have been periodically bolstered by separate IMF borrowing arrangements with members, on a temporary basis, such as the 1974-75 oil facility. In addition, the IMF acts as trustee for a legally separate trust fund which it manages on behalf of members. (The various facilities are discussed in more detail in Chapter Six.)

The basic structure is the same in the Amended Articles but the nomenclature is now changed. The General Account is renamed the General Department and the Special Drawing Account is now called the Special Drawing Rights Department. The General Department will consist of three separate accounts — the General Resources Account to administer the resources previously held in the General Account, the Special Disbursement Account to hold profits on future IMF gold sales under Article V, 12, and the Investment Account to hold the resources used for and resulting from investment. The IMF is also authorised, under Amended Article V, 2, to perform 'financial and technical services, including the administration of resources contributed by members, that are consistent with the purposes of the Fund'. These accounts are analysed more fully in Chapter Seven.

Membership

The central role of the IMF reflects its wide membership (132 countries in April 1978) which excludes only Switzerland and the bulk of the Socialist bloc. The main barrier to the latter countries has been IMF Article VIII, 5, which obliges members to furnish the Fund with detailed information on their balance of payments, international reserves, international investments, national income, prices and exchange controls. However, there have been indications from time to time that Poland (which left the IMF in 1948), Hungary and Czechoslovakia might be interested in joining, presumably with the approval of the USSR. Exploratory discussions took place with Poland in 1977 but the intentions of these Eastern European countries have yet to be seriously tested.

In spite of the efforts of Keynes and others, the IMF has never been the all-powerful arbiter of international finance often depicted by wayward governments. Real decisions are taken by national authorities in the light of their own national interests and only then is a consensus sought in the Fund. Power in this area reflects economic and political power generally and the special position of the United States has never been effectively challenged. The United States has by far the largest quota (i.e. the largest subscription to IMF resources) and the largest voting share, some

20% in 1978, which gives an effective veto on important measures. The United States has also contributed significantly to IMF borrowing operations such as the 1962 General Arrangements to Borrow. The dollar has always accounted for a high proportion of the currencies which the Fund can use in its lending and US influence has been further strengthened by the development of the dollar as the major trading and reserve currency since 1945.

On the whole, US power has been exercised with restraint. It has not always carried the day, the best example being December 1971 when a dollar devaluation was forced on a very reluctant US Administration. However, it has meant that the United States has always enjoyed considerable freedom in economic policymaking, interference in which by any international organisation has seldom had much impact. In the 1960s the IMF had no power to call the United States to account for the persistent large scale payments' deficits which ultimately brought about the suspension of dollar convertibility into gold in 1971. In the late 1970s the IMF is still very much constrained by the independent stance of the United States.

Organisation

The official governing body of the Fund is the Board of Governors, a rather unwieldy assembly representing all Fund members at finance minister and central bank governor level. The Board meets once a year at the annual meetings which are an important occasion for numerous informal contacts even though the resolutions passed do little more than ratify formally what is decided elsewhere. Proposals to establish advisory committees or to hold more frequent half-yearly meetings have foundered on the problems of convening so large a group and of determining its terms of reference. Most decisions of the Board of Governors are taken through the post: votes are sent to the Fund on individual resolutions.

In the interests of efficiency, the Board of Governors has authority to delegate most of its powers to the Executive Directors under both the pre-1978 and the Amended Articles. The Board can, however, withdraw a power that has been delegated or reverse a decision by the Executive Directors, taken under a delegated power, whenever it sees fit. The Original Articles reserved certain powers to the Board of Governors which concerned political issues, such as the admission of new members, or measures with far-reaching effects on the international monetary system, such as the allocation of SDRs. Other reserved powers involved delicate questions such as the distribution of Fund income. All these decisions affected the membership as a whole and, in contrast to the usual Executive Directors' procedure, were subject to a special majority of the voting power.

In the Amended Articles the distribution and delegation of powers has been further clarified (Amended Article XII). Powers are now classified into two groups: those directly conferred on the Board of Governors, the Council, the Executive Directors or the Managing Director, and those vested in the Board of Governors which may be delegated to the Executive Directors or the Council at the Board of Governors' discretion. As previously, the powers reserved to the Board of Governors are confined to those with a special institutional importance in the Fund. Again, as before, these decisions will normally require a special majority of 70% or 85% of the voting power.

The other decision-making organ of the Fund is the Executive Board which is drawn from the intermediate levels of members' civil services and central banks. The Executive Board currently has twenty members (Executive Directors), five of whom are appointed by the members with the largest quotas, the United States, the United Kingdom, West Germany, France and Japan. The other fifteen are elected every two years by the remaining members grouped into constituencies, consisting of countries with common interests, which in practice have been fairly stable.

The size of the Executive Board (originally twelve) is governed by considerations of efficiency and the need to maintain an appropriate geographical balance between the constituencies. It is also generally accepted that the size of the constituencies should be restricted to avoid placing undue burdens on Executive Directors. These considerations lay behind the provision in the Original Articles that Latin and Central America should have three Directors and the understanding, in 1972, that the sub-Saharan African countries should be represented by two directors. Despite protests against under-representation the developing countries account for nine of the twenty seats.

The present number of Executive Directors has been incorporated into the Amended Articles but there is provision for it to be changed by an 85% majority vote in the Board of Governors. A member not entitled to appoint its own Executive Director retains the right to send a representative to the Executive Board 'when a request made by, or a matter particularly affecting, that member is under consideration' (Amended Article XII,3(j)). Also retained is the provision for two additional directors to be appointed if the five appointed directors do not include those two members that have made available the largest absolute amounts of resources used by the Fund in its General Account operations 'on the average over the two years preceding a regular election of Executive Directors' (Amended Article XII, 3(c)). In the Original Articles this provision was mandatory but it is optional under the Amended Articles, to avoid disrupting previously agreed constituency groupings. It remains a potentially important way of giving major new creditors a stronger voice in Fund management. Although it has been used only once, by Canada in 1958-60, it should be applied to Saudi Arabia in the 1978 elections, which could have the important effect of linking OPEC more closely to the present international financial system.

The Executive Board is responsible for the day-to-day running of the Fund. According to an IMF decision in 1948, its function is 'to determine and formulate the policies of the Fund and to make decisions concerning major problems of the Fund'. It is distinguished by two special features. Firstly, the Executive Board is in continuous session, which enables governments to exercise a closer control over the Fund's general operations than is normally the case with international organisations. (From 1972-1975, for example, there were an average of over 100 meetings a year.) Secondly, the Executive Board operates under a system of weighted voting: the voting strength of each Executive Director is based on the quotas of the member or members which appointed or elected him. Each member has a basic allocation of 250 votes plus one vote for every SDR 100,000 of quota. Although this has led to periodic complaints, not just from developing countries, against oligarchic procedures, it is the way in which the IMF avoids the lack of realism which sometimes characterises the United Nations and other world bodies. It is inconceivable, for example, that major creditors would, or should, be bound by 'democratic' financial decisions.

The Executive Directors cast the votes of their constituents as one unit, although they are free to express all their differing positions or to abstain in the last resort. Decisions are usually taken by a simple majority of the votes cast (Amended Article XII, 5(c)), and the pre-1978 Articles only required special majorities in six instances — one by a majority of the total voting power, one by a two-thirds majority, two by a 75% majority and two by unanimous vote. These majorities owed as much to political compromise as to logic, and Gold (1972), the IMF's legal adviser, admitted that it was not always possible to explain with certainty why a particular proportion of the total voting power was chosen or why different proportions were adopted for the various categories of decision.

Under the Amended Articles the categories of special majorities in the Executive Board (and in the Board of Governors) are reduced to two — 85% for major decisions and 70% for non-routine decisions of slightly less importance. On the other hand the total number of decisions subject to special majorities has been increased to 52 (with 14 of these coming under powers reserved to the Board of Governors). The increase reflects the inability to agree on fundamental reforms in the 1972-1976 discussions, which made it necessary to include various possible courses of action in key areas.

In practice this need not be a major stumbling-block, since the Executive Board has tended to work by consensus which takes into account the views of smaller countries. Widespread support is always sought for important decisions, special majority or no, and the avoidance of voting has helped to maintain the cohesion of the IMF as an institution, notwithstanding the diversity of economic interests among members. A more important drawback has been the relatively junior level of representation on the Executive Board which has limited its decision-making capacity on really major issues. Strategic principles have tended to come from higher level meetings of smaller groups of countries such as the Group of Ten. The initial decisions on the SDR in the mid-1960s, for example, were taken in the latter forum, while the exchange rate provisions of the Amended Articles were decided by a Franco-American compromise at the Rambouillet Summit in November 1975. Nonetheless the Executive Board often does the groundwork for important decisions; and its report in 1972 on international monetary reform anticipated much of the Committee of Twenty's deliberations.

The Managing Director is the non-voting chairman of the Executive Board. According to the Articles he is elected by the Executive Board, but in practice it is an important political appointment in which governments are closely involved. By tradition the Managing Director has been a prominent European official or politician (while the President of the World Bank has been an American).

To date there have been five Managing Directors, and Witteveen — the present incumbent — retires in 1978. The Managing Director has an important role as spokesman for the Fund on matters of adjustment and reform, and certain powers are reserved to him in the Articles, notably the right to propose allocations or cancellations of SDRs (Amended Article XVIII, 4). To a large extent the maintenance of Fund influence in recent years has been the result of Witteveen's personal contribution towards pushing through the Amended Articles and negotiating new credit lines to supplement Fund resources.

A new development since 1974 has been the establishment of an Interim Committee of Governors whose function has been to supervise the transition from the present to a reformed international monetary system. As its name suggests, the Interim Committee was intended as a bridge between the 1972-74 Committee of Twenty (C20), the forum for the reform discussions, and a permanent Council of Governors which can be brought into being by an 85% majority of the Board of Governors under Amended Article XII, 1.   The Council will have the same terms of reference as the Interim Committee, namely the management and adaptation of the international monetary system, including surveillance of members' adjustment and liquidity arrangements, with the crucial distinction that the Council will have decision-making powers where the Interim Committee, like the C20, has a purely advisory role.

The Council, like the Interim Committee, will be composed of finance ministers and central bank governors; and similarly the members, twenty in all, will be drawn from the same constituencies as the Executive Board.   This format has proved reasonably effective in the ten or so Interim Committee meetings held to date.   It is sufficiently high-level, compact and representative to take important decisions, such as the January 1976 temporary enlargement of the first credit tranche.   However, the Interim Committee has been handicapped by the absence of an agreed adjustment framework and this will be one of the pre-conditions for the Council's establishment and, more importantly, its effective operation.

CHAPTER TWO

THE BRETTON WOODS SYSTEM 1944 - 73

The system created at Bretton Woods did not operate in the manner envisaged by its architects. The shortcomings of the original structure were exposed after 1960 by inflationary pressures in the major countries, prolonged balance of payments deficit in the United States (and a consequent surplus of dollars in the rest of the world) and a far greater than expected volume of capital movements. Ultimately these developments led to the crises of August 1971 and March 1973 and to the Committee of Twenty's abortive attempt at wholesale international monetary reform after September 1972. The Committee's failure means that many of the problems analysed below remain unsolved.

The system established at Bretton Woods was based on four main pillars which endowed the Fund with broad regulatory powers as follows:

(1)　co-operation in international monetary affairs;
(2)　freedom of current account transactions;
(3)　provision of 'sufficient' international liquidity through monetary gold and IMF quotas; and
(4)　maintenance of 'stable but adjustable' par values for exchange rates.

See 51 pg2.

Co-operation

In this respect the Fund was generally successful, although the co-operation was at times reserved and the IMF management was not sufficiently forward-looking to prevent the ultimate breakdown of the system. Co-operation was sometimes confined to an inner circle of industrial members and real decisions were often taken in this 'Group of Ten' which usually met before IMF meetings to agree a common position. At the same time the establishment of Working Party Number 3 by the Economic Policy Committee of the OECD in 1961 provided a more compact forum at a more senior level than the IMF Executive Board for the discussion of policy harmonisation among industrial countries

Freedom of current account transactions

Article VIII of the 1944 Agreement obliged members to avoid restrictions on current payments and to avoid discriminatory currency practices. A special exemptions procedure (Original Article XIV) allowed countries to retain restrictions for what was expected to be a transitional period. At first only the United States and some Latin

American countries fully accepted Article VIII obligations but they were followed by Canada in 1952, the United Kingdom and other Western European countries in 1961 and Japan in 1964. The IMF was also successful in encouraging the elimination, on a wider scale, of bilateral trade agreements and multiple exchange rate practices (that is, more favourable rates for certain transactions). Yet Article XIV has continued to be useful in justifying restrictions necessarily imposed by developing countries. Its provisions still cover roughly two-thirds of IMF members and they have been retained in the Amended Articles.

In contrast to current account transactions, Original Article VI specifically exempted members' capital transfers from the requirements of Article VIII. Members were permitted, and in some cases actually encouraged, to prevent capital movements for fear of their disruptive effects. (These provisions have not been changed in the Amended Articles.) In practice, however, at least until the mid-1960s, the major countries which had made their currencies convertible also moved in the direction of liberalising capital transfers.

International liquidity

The designers of the Bretton Woods system assumed that international settlements would be in gold, supplemented where necessary by credit from the IMF. The necessary growth in international reserves over time would be achieved through new monetary gold entering the system and periodic increases in IMF quotas. In practice, however, the United States alone undertook to convert its currency into gold at a fixed price (Original Article IV, 4) and dollar convertibility made it convenient for other countries to use dollars in international settlements and to hold dollars, which earned interest (unlike gold), in their reserves. At the same time the need for reserves, consequent on the growth in world trade after 1945, considerably exceeded the stock of monetary gold and IMF quotas. As a result global liquidity requirements were met in dollars through successive United States balance of payments deficits.

This arrangement worked satisfactorily before 1960 when the economic dominance of the United States was unquestioned and confidence in the dollar was high. The amounts involved were relatively small and helped to finance the post-war European economic recovery. Surplus countries were therefore content to hold dollar liabilities without conversion. In the 1960s, however, the United States moved into a heavy and persistent balance of payments deficit, and other countries' holdings of dollars grew out of all proportion to US gold reserves. Not surprisingly, confidence in the commitment of the United States to gold convertibility was seriously undermined and the situation was not helped by disagreement over whether the deficit indicated a fundamental disequilibrium in the US economy or a shortage of international reserves in the system. There were those like McKinnon — as Williamson (1973) records — who maintained that the deficit reflected 'mutually beneficial financial intermediation': it was not a symptom of domestic indiscipline but rather a product of the rest of the world's demand for liquidity. But this argument ignored the responsiveness of the deficit, at least in the short to medium term, to changes in US domestic monetary policy.

Two things were certain, the growing instability of the gold exchange standard and the powerlessness of the IMF to bring pressure to bear on the United States to alter its domestic policies.   Eventually the dollar became a less attractive asset to hold than gold, which led to massive speculation against the dollar at the least sign of crisis.   Under the Washington Agreement in March 1968 the central banks' 'gold pool', formed in 1961 with the object of maintaining the market price of gold in the close vicinity of the official price, was abandoned and a two-tier gold market separating the free market from the official market was estab-lished.   Certain understandings were formalised among the major countries, restricting the conversion of dollars into gold by the United States. Although the polite fiction was maintained, until August 1971, that gold was still 'freely sold' against the dollar, the right of convertibility depended increasingly on its not being exercised — that is, on the deliberate restraint of the major trading partners of the United States.

The weakness of the dollar also highlighted the shortage, existing and prospective, of other 'safer' forms of international liquidity, evident in the adjustment problems of major countries and the widespread imposition of trade and payments restrictions.   But, although there was general agreement after 1960 on the need to increase world reserves, the amount and the form of such an increase were more controversial issues. Considerable problems were involved in any attempt to quantify the demand for, or determine the optimum supply of, world reserves and they remain unsolved.   On the demand side, as Williamson (1973) has shown, mixed results were obtained from empirical models.   Simple formulae linking the level of reserves to imports failed to allow for arbitrary factors such as confidence, which prompted Machlup's entertaining theory, mentioned by Williamson (1973), that the attitude of central bankers to reserves resem-bled that of a woman to her wardrobe — both were happy if they acquired a little more each year.   With regard to supply there were at least three recognised approaches concentrating respectively on 'welfare maximisation', 'target reconciliation' and 'price stabilisation'.   Not surprisingly Fleming, as noted by Williamson (1973), stressed the 'multiplicity of targets' and the 'paucity of effective instruments' in this area.

In the 1960s the solutions to the liquidity problem fell into two broad categories, those which left the basic structure of the system unchanged and those which envisaged the creation of new forms of world reserves.

(a)   Temporary expedients

In the first category, provision was made in the Original IMF Articles for a 'uniform change in par values' (Original Article IV, 7), that is, a change in the official price of gold against all currencies together.   In theory it enabled countries to write up (or write down) the value of their gold reserves by a similar proportion, but it was never used. Apart from the political problems in obtaining agreement for such a step, it was widely opposed on the grounds that it would lead to an arbitrary division of new liquidity and encourage destabilising speculation in anti-cipation of future increases.   It would certainly have failed to provide for a steady growth of world reserves in line with increasing demand.

In practice the gold exchange standard was kept going by what Halm (1971) called 'a flowering of ingenious credit arrangements' among the major countries.   Depending on one's point of view, they could be taken as signs of the system's adaptability or its inherent weakness.   As well as emergency bilateral credits, the *ad hoc* arrangements included an elaborate network of central bank swap facilities, large increases in IMF quotas and the establishment of the General Arrangements to Borrow.

The swap network was set up by the Federal Reserve Bank of New York (FRBNY) in 1961-62 and is still in active use today. It consists of bilateral agreements, totalling some $22 billion, with fourteen developed countries and the Bank for International Settlements.

Table 2.1   Swap arrangements with the FRBNY

$ million

Austrian National Bank	250	Bank of Japan	2,000
National Bank of Belgium	1,000	Bank of Mexico	180
Bank of Canada	2,000	Netherlands Bank	500
National Bank of Denmark	250	Bank of Norway	250
Bank of England	3,000	Bank of Sweden	300
Bank of France	2,000	Swiss National Bank	1,400
German Federal Bank	4,000[1]	Bank for International	
Bank of Italy	3,000	Settlements	1,850

Source: *Federal Reserve Bank of New York Monthly Bulletin*

[1] Amount doubled to $4 billion in March 1978

The swaps are usually for three months but are renewable. They are virtually unconditional, but drawings on the Federal Reserve Bank of New York are subject to close scrutiny by Congress. In the 1960s the facility was activated on several occasions, notably by the Bank of England, but it was intended purely as a defence against short-term monetary disturbances — nothing more.

The General Arrangements to Borrow (GAB) were established by the major industrial countries (the Group of Ten) and Switzerland (listed in Table 2.2) in 1961-62 under the replenishment provisions of IMF Article VII, 2. The initial arrangement was for five years and has since been renewed three times. Commitments, expressed in national currencies, totalled $6 billion in 1961 dollars and, in the words of the relevant Executive Board decision in October 1962, were primarily intended to provide the IMF with:

> 'supplementary resources to forestall or cope with an impairment of the international monetary system [arising from] the new conditions of widespread convertibility, including greater freedom for short-term capital movements'.

The total was based on the largest drawings from the IMF by the two reserve centres, the United States and the United Kingdom, which could then reasonably be envisaged. Country shares were decided by straightforward bargaining: in the case of the United Kingdom, prestige and a large voting power were as important as the possible need to meet an exceptional demand for sterling in the IMF.

Table 2.2   The GAB: Original contributions

	1961 $ million	National currencies	
Belgium	150	BFcs	7,500,000,000
Canada	200	Can $	208,938,000
Deutsche Bundesbank	1,000	DM	4,000,000,000
France	550	Fr Fcs	2,715,381,428
Italy	550	Lit	343,750,000,000
Japan	250	Yen	90,000,000,000
Netherlands	200	Fl	724,000,000
Sveriges Riksbank	100	Sw Kr	517,320,000
UK	1,000	£	357,142,587
US	2,000	US$	2,000,000,000
Total	6,000		
Plus		*Plus*	
Switzerland		Sw Fcs	865,000,000

Source: *IMF Survey*, 10 January 1977

The arrangement essentially consists of commitments by the Group of Ten (G.10) to lend up to a specified amount of their currencies to the IMF when it is needed to finance drawings, subject to the usual tranche conditions, by other G.10 members.   Commitments can only be used by the IMF to cover G.10 drawings, and each activation of the GAB requires a formal proposal from the IMF Managing Director, consultations in the Executive Board and the support of at least six GAB participants accounting for 60% of total commitments.   Contributors and the size of individual contributions are chosen with reference to the relative balance of payments, reserves and IMF positions of participants.   There is provision for the transfer of loans to other participants if a creditor's economic position worsens.   Interest on GAB loans was originally paid by the IMF in gold at a rate of 1½% per annum, but since October 1975 the rate has been 4% rising in line with the charges on the associated drawing from the IMF.

The arrangement has proved a useful backstop to IMF lending.   In the ten years to 1972 it was used on seven occasions, chiefly by the United Kingdom and France, for a total of SDR 2.2 billion, all repaid by August 1971.   However, the commitments have not been increased to match rising needs and by the mid-1970s had fallen below their original level as a result of currency devaluations by participants.   In the 1960s they provided, at best, a temporary palliative which did not solve the problems caused by loss of confidence in the reserve currency system.

(b)   Radical reform

There was no lack of proposals — well summarised by Williamson (1973) — for a new fiduciary reserve asset.   Chief among them were the

Hart, Kaldor, Tinbergen proposal for a commodity reserve currency; the Stamp Plan, under which the IMF would issue certificates to the IBRD for allocation to LDCs; and Bernstein's Composite Reserve Units (CRUs) which would be issued to major countries in exchange for currency and used to supplement gold in settlements within this group. Equally radical was Triffin's scheme for the transfer of reserve currency liabilities to the IMF in exchange for Fund deposits carrying a gold guarantee; the Fund would be authorised to expand these deposits at an agreed annual rate (say 3%) through open market operations in member countries, gold sales and investment in IBRD bonds. The IMF would become an international central bank able to hold deposits and create credit.

The various proposals, like those of Keynes twenty years before, proved too extreme for the financially orthodox industrial countries. None was without certain drawbacks. The Kaldor/Tinbergen plan would have turned the IMF into an international stockpiling agency, quite apart from the impracticality of having an ultimate reserve asset based on perishable commodities. The Stamp plan assumed, without justification, that the IMF was prepared to act as a development institution and relied too heavily on the major countries' voluntary acceptance of unknown certificates in payment by LDCs. The flaw in the proposal for CRUs was their limited scope, since their use and their benefits would have been confined to a small group of industrial countries. Not unnaturally this was resented by countries outside the Group of Ten, a resentment which found expression in the assertion by Schweitzer, then Managing Director of the IMF, that international liquidity was 'the business of the Fund'. Moreover, Triffin's ideas presupposed a unanimity over the IMF's role — conspicuously lacking both then and now. His scheme left open the possibility of a run on the IMF, particularly if the Fund's assets were backed mainly by developing country debts.

In view of the number of alternatives, the unquantifiable economic factors, the immense technical problems and the deep-rooted national differences of opinion, it was of major significance that the SDR or any international reserve asset was created at all. The SDR scheme, negotiated within the IMF in 1965-69, represented the first concerted attempt to influence world reserves through the introduction of a fiduciary instrument (i.e. not backed by 'real' assets) dependent for its acceptability solely on the confidence of users in the issuing authority. Decisions to allocate and cancel SDRs were to be subject to high voting majorities and to be taken for five year 'basic periods', running consecutively from the date of the first allocation (although the first basic period was only three years, 1970-72). Total allocations were to be based on the 'long term global need ... to supplement existing reserve assets' and individual country shares determined in proportion to quotas. Nearly all IMF members chose to become 'participants' in the scheme.

Inevitably the SDR was a compromise — economic, political and legal. On the one hand it was endowed with asset-like characteristics, such as the assurance of unchallengeable use through an obligation on participants to accept SDRs for currency, which made the SDR legally superior to gold as a means of international payment. The Articles ensured that participants using SDRs would receive an 'equal value' of currency in exchange at representative rates irrespective of the currency provided or the participant providing it. The value of the SDR was defined in terms of gold (0.888671 grammes) and it was given a modest interest rate, 1½%, as an inducement for participants to hold SDRs in excess of their allocations. The low interest rate assumed, not unreasonably given the evidence of 1945-67, that the gold-denominated SDR would appreciate against currencies in general. Equally important, as pointed out by Gold (1970), world interest rates were comparatively low in the late 1960s and the United States was unwilling to allow the SDR to compete with the dollar.

On the other hand, several restrictive features were incorporated at the insistence of European creditors, notably France. Participants were only allowed to use SDRs (i.e. exchange them for currency) if they could establish a balance of payments or reserve need, subject to IMF authorisation, and not for the purpose of 'changing the composition' of their reserves. Use was initially limited to three kinds of official (non-private) transaction — between participants and the IMF General Account, between participants and 'prescribed other holders' (which so far only numbers the Bank for International Settlements) and between participants themselves. In the last mentioned case participants use SDRs by agreement or by designation — whereby participants are able to exchange SDRs for the currency of other participants designated by the IMF. Quarterly designation plans are prepared by the IMF on the basis of participants' balance of payments and reserve strengths, with the aim of avoiding haphazard or inequitable distribution of SDRs over time.

But perhaps the single most important internal deterrent to wider use of SDRs has been the reconstitution provisions. They were included, at French insistence, as a safeguard against the employment of SDRs to meet prolonged payments deficits. They require participants to recon- stitute (i.e. restore) their SDR holdings such that 'five years after the first allocation, and at the end of each calendar quarter thereafter, the average of their daily holdings over the most recent five year period will not be less than 30% of their daily net cumulative allocations of SDRs over the same period'. The necessary calculations are done by the Fund; and participants which fall below the 30% minimum are designated to acquire SDRs for currency from other participants in the quarterly plans. Participants are also expected to pay 'due regard' to the pursuit of a 'balanced relationship' over time between their holdings of SDRs and other forms of international reserves.

Not surprisingly, the reconstitution provisions are strongly resented by many participants since only 70% of SDR allocations can effectively be treated as owned reserves. More generally, the dual nature of the SDR — reserve asset and conditional drawing right — has hampered its development as the principal reserve asset of the international monetary system. This aspect is examined more fully in Chapters Three and Seven.

In theory the advent of SDRs meant that US payments' deficits were no longer essential to world liquidity needs. The system was given a new element of flexibility whereby the United States would ultimately be able to act not as world banker but like any large country. The catch was twofold, first that the US deficit was entrenched by 1969-70 and second that SDRs were created as a supplement (and not a substitute) to existing reserve assets. According to Hirsch (1976):

> 'SDRs did not replace dollars — they were intended by the
> US authorities rather to shore up the dollar. They did not
> replace gold — they were accepted by European countries as
> a minor form of diversifying the paper component of reserves'.

SDRs did not limit the freedom of countries to choose the composition of their reserves and neither did they have any influence on the supply of international reserves in other forms. In consequence, SDRs could not serve their intended purpose of controlling the total level of world reserves or replacing the dollar as the principal reserve asset. The initial allocations of SDR 9.3 billion in 1970-72 were based on Fund estimates of a rising world demand for reserves of SDR 4-5 billion per annum and an increase of only SDR 1.0-1.5 billion in the annual supply of other reserve assets. Instead they were accompanied by an unprecedented increase in the US deficit (caused by Vietnam War expenditure), a tripling of world foreign exchange reserves (+SDR 63 billion), mainly in the form of dollars held directly or through the euromarkets, and two-figure global inflation. At end-1972 SDRs accounted for only 10% of the world's liquid reserves excluding gold.

After 1970, therefore, the 'dollar problem' remained in even more acute form. In retrospect there may be some truth in Mundell's criticism of SDRs — recorded by Williamson (1973) — as a diversionary tactic which distracted attention from other more fundamental weaknesses of the system. In August 1971 the fundamental imbalance in major currency relationships, caused by chronic basic deficit in the United States and persistent surplus in Western European countries and Japan, prompted the formal suspension of dollar/gold convertibility and with it the demise of the gold exchange standard.

Par values

The other main prop of the Bretton Woods agreement was the system of parity values for currencies whereby exchange rates were fixed but adjustable. Parity rates for given units of currency were expressed in terms of a weight of gold and countries were obliged to keep the spot rate for their currencies within margins of 1% either side of parity (Original Article IV). This they might do either by electing to 'freely buy and sell' gold at the appropriate price for their currency or by intervening as necessary in their own exchange market. Only the United States opted to use the first of these methods, and the dollar became the principal currency used by governments when intervening to support the parities of their own currencies.

The right to propose an exchange rate adjustment was reserved to the member country alone but the IMF retained the right to accept or reject the proposal. The criterion for making an adjustment was the existence, in the judgement of the Fund, of a 'fundamental disequilibrium', never precisely defined, in the economy of the member concerned. In many cases exchange market pressures turned the necessary consultation with the Fund into a formal endorsement after the event. The Fund only once objected to a proposed change by a major country (France in 1948) and then because it was linked to multiple currency practices.

In theory, the 'discipline' of fixed parities was combined with the 'safety valve' of parity changes if external (balance of payments) equilibrium at fixed exchange rates required either too much inflation or too much unemployment in member countries. The principle was established that exchange rates were a matter of international rather than purely national concern: and the IMF was there to assist members with finance and advice during the period of adjustment to new parities.

Until the early 1960s the par value system worked without obvious strains, mainly because there was little policy conflict between the major countries and also because the liberalisation of capital flows was a gradual process.   Yet the benefits of par values were not perhaps as clear-cut as was commonly supposed.   It is hard, if not impossible, for example, to isolate the exact contribution of the exchange rate system to the unparalleled growth of world trade in this period, quite apart from identifying whether the major contribution came from having fixed points of reference or from the possibility of exchange rate changes as a last resort.   The system evidently failed to prevent periodic crises after 1963 which necessitated the adoption of 'temporary' trade restrictions by industrial countries, notably the United Kingdom, and an elaborate network of controls and multiple exchange rates in many developing countries.

It would also be misleading to credit the par value régime with the virtual freedom from competitive exchange rate depreciation (i.e. devaluation) since 1945.   The likelihood of this happening was considerably reduced by the generally successful implementation of domestic demand management policies in major countries, policies which might have been equally successful under a different exchange rate system.   A far greater problem in the 1960s was posed by countries postponing devaluation until alternative policies, and foreign exchange reserves, were exhausted.

Similarly, the claim by the IMF Executive Directors (1970) that fixed exchange rates performed the functions of the price mechanism in influencing the allocation of resources and contributing to the balance of supply and demand should be treated with caution.   In some cases the adoption of unrealistic parities interfered with the exchange market price mechanism, necessitating more or less continuous intervention and comprehensive exchange controls.   The consequent distortions justified Halm's comments (1971) that a price system with 'wrong prices' might conceivably be even worse than a system that 'stops relying on prices altogether'.

Perhaps the major claim of conservative commentators, and central bankers in particular, was that par values provided a useful discipline for the maintenance of domestic financial stability.   By implication,the possibility alone of devaluation would normally be sufficient to ensure internal corrective action and promote political willingness to impose unpopular restraints.   Even where the attempt to defend the parity ultimately failed, the 'psychological shock' of devaluation would produce support for the associated measures necessary to curtail domestic demand. As late as 1970 the IMF Executive Directors were agreed that stable but adjustable par values comprised the most appropriate exchange rate régime in a world of managed national economies.

But these last claims can be challenged.   They presupposed, in many cases wrongly, that par values were set at realistic levels: and they elevated defence of an exchange rate into an end in itself irrespective of changes in members' relative economic positions.   At the same time the IMF concept of 'fundamental disequilibrium' left open the possibility of rate changes which weakened the various attempts at policy co-ordination among the major countries in the 1960s;   and the *ad hoc* financing arrangements in this period allowed countries to avoid, at least partially and often only temporarily, the much vaunted discipline on their domestic economies.

In the 1960s these contradictions became increasingly apparent. There were signs, for example in the United Kingdom, that the defence of fixed rates was carried beyond the point where it served the wider interests of the country and, arguably, of the system itself. However, there was no agreement on appropriate methods of adjustment, mainly because devaluation, contrary to what was intended at Bretton Woods, came to be regarded as a last resort crisis measure. The concept of 'fundamental disequilibrium' was interpreted very restrictively in the 1960s, to the extent that it almost acted as a barrier to exchange rate adjustment. In 1970, for example, it was defined by the IMF Executive Directors as 'a situation in which external and internal considerations are pulling in opposite directions as regards domestic stabilisation measures ... and where this conflict is of a persistent nature'. Even in this dilemma, other measures to restore payments balance 'should be preferred' to exchange rate adjustment.

Between 1949 and 1967 only two major countries, excluding Canada which floated in 1950-62, used a par value change as a mechanism for adjustment. They were France, which devalued in 1956 and 1958, and West Germany which revalued in 1961. Exchange rate changes were, according to Williamson (1977), relegated to the status of confessions that the adjustment process had failed.. Flexibility was limited to smaller countries and even here, as Cooper (1971) has shown, it was associated with political loss of face and very often loss of job for the finance ministers concerned.

Equally important there was no agreement on the criteria indicating a country's need or responsibility to adjust. The lack of such criteria produced real conflicts between the United States and the rest of the world and between surplus and deficit countries. The position of the United States was complicated by two factors. It was the only country to fulfil its obligations under IMF Article IV by freely buying and selling gold which made the dollar the *de facto* numeraire of the system: and the dollar also became the main reserve asset, as explained above. It was widely assumed, wrongly as the 1971 Smithsonian agreement proved, that the United States was not free to alter its par value. In the 1960s this left other countries with the main burden, and cost, of initiating exchange rate changes even though it was the competitive position of the United States which had weakened. Conversely, as Katz (1972) has shown, there is some evidence, not conclusive, that the dollar appreciated against currencies in general between 1959 and 1969 despite the persistent payments deficits of the United States and periodic capital outflows.

A further asymmetry was apparent in the different pressures on surplus and deficit countries. There were no effective means of disciplining surplus countries in the IMF Articles. Even in theory the Fund's powers, set out in the 'scarce currency' clauses of the Original Article VII, were limited. In the case of a general scarcity of a currency, resulting from a chronic external surplus in one country, the Fund was merely authorised to issue a report with recommendations to end the scarcity. If a scarcity developed in the Fund's holdings of a currency, the Fund was empowered to ration that currency in its operations, to declare the currency formally scarce and to allow the imposition of temporary exchange restrictions on the scarce currency country by other members.

However, these sanctions were never used, partly because the scarcity of a currency was thought to be a fallible guide to the need for adjustment and partly because of a general reluctance to sanction restrictions in what was intended to be a liberal system. In the period of

dollar shortage between 1945 and 1960 the clauses could technically have
been applied against the United States: but this would have been nonsensi-
cal in view of the tremendous efforts made by that country, notably through
Marshall Aid, to rebuild the economies of Europe and Japan.   In the case
of other currencies the question of scarcity was very hard to define since
none was used in Fund transactions on anything like the scale of the dollar.
The establishment of the GAB in 1962 confirmed the dead letter status of
these restrictions by enabling surplus countries to lend additional amounts
of their currency to the Fund, thus avoiding the possibility of a technical scarcity.

In theory surplus countries were supposed to use revaluation as a
way of protecting their economies from imported inflation: but, although
there were five revaluations by major countries between 1959 and 1970,
which was remarkable on past standards, the surplus nations were also
guilty of 'competitive fixity'.   Revaluation was avoided as long as possible, to benefit export industries, and capital inflows were partly neutral-
ised by conservative fiscal and monetary policies.   Exchange rate changes
were left to the 'sick' rather than the 'healthy', a philosophy which the
IMF could do little about.

Deficit countries were subject to much greater pressures.   They
were more likely to be forced into devaluation by loss of reserves which
were finite, whereas there was no apparent limit to the accumulation of
reserves by countries such as West Germany and Japan.   International
borrowing was temporary and conditional, imposing further economic and
political constraints.   The failure to devalue was accompanied by the
prospect of permanent loss of export markets.   When a country eventually
devalued, it often did so by the maximum amount possible in order to
encourage capital inflows and avoid the suspicion of a second devaluation.

The resulting patchwork of undervalued and overvalued currencies
was inevitably exploited by the owners of short-term mobile capital, mainly
international financial institutions and trading companies.   The mobility
of these flows stemmed from several factors: the increasing integration
of the post-war international economy; the emergence after 1960 of large
scale balance of payments disequilibria together with relatively wide
interest rate disparities among financial centres; and the greater likelihood of parity changes following the 1967 devaluation of sterling.   The
system of stable but adjustable par values had no defence, short of
exchange controls more stringent than most countries could accept, against
this kind of speculation.   It was always obvious in which direction a
change would be made, so that the owners of short-term capital could make
one-way bets.   By 1970-71 capital mobility had developed on a scale
sufficient to deprive governments of the freedom to choose the timing and
the scope of their adjustment policies.

The collapse of the dollar/gold exchange standard in August 1971
did not of itself bring down the system of stable but adjustable par
values.   It was, in fact, restored by the Smithsonian agreement of
December 1971 which provided the first multilateral realignment of
exchange rates among the major countries, based on reasonably sophisticated calculations of adjustment needs.   The realignment included a 7.9%
devaluation of the dollar, a revaluation of the yen and the Deutschemark
and no change in the value of sterling or the French franc in terms of the
SDR.   The pattern of changes was quickly followed by adaptations of the
exchange rate policies of many developing countries which resulted, on
average, in a moderate depreciation of their currencies in relation to

those of the developed countries.   Most countries moved in the same
direction as their main trading partners, which lessened the impact of
parity changes on effective (that is trade-weighted) exchange rates.
Overall the value of the SDR and of reserve positions in the Fund (i.e.
currencies held by the Fund at below 75% of members' quotas) was approximately unchanged in relation to the major currencies in general.

President Nixon's unfortunate description of the Smithsonian
accords as 'the greatest monetary agreement in the history of the world'
has tended to obscure other equally important aspects of the 1971
arrangements.   Not only was the SDR used as numeraire for the parity
changes, but the dollar was treated exactly like other currencies,
contrary to the original intentions of the US Government.   At the same
time the IMF inaugurated a 'temporary' measure of greater exchange rate
flexibility in the form of central rates and wider margins.   Members
were permitted to maintain a 'stable (central) rate' for their currencies
in terms of an intervention currency, nearly always the dollar, as one
way of fulfilling their exchange obligations.   Such rates could be
communicated to the Fund in gold, SDR or another member's currency.
Exchange rates, in transactions between a member's currency and its
intervention currency, were allowed to move within margins of $2\frac{1}{4}$%
(formerly 1%) on either side of the parity relationship as indicated by
their par values or central rates.   As a result maximum margins of $4\frac{1}{2}$%
(formerly 2%) were possible in relation to other currencies.

In the longer term the Smithsonian agreement also provided the
impetus to more far-reaching reform.   The Group of Ten participants were
unanimous that discussions on this subject should be undertaken promptly
within the framework of the IMF.   In the short term, however, the attempt
to preserve stable but adjustable par values was frustrated by an unprecedented increase in world inflation, accompanied by widening inflation
differentials and larger payments' imbalance between countries.   The
necessity of more frequent parity adjustments exacerbated the problem of
capital movements on a massive scale.   In June 1972 the pound sterling
was floated and this was followed by the second devaluation of the
dollar in February 1973 and the joint float of EEC currencies in March
1973.   By then the authorities in the major countries were no longer
willing or able to shore up an exchange rate system which ultimately
imposed insupportable burdens on their reserves and domestic policies.

CHAPTER THREE

THE FAILURE OF INTERNATIONAL MONETARY REFORM

The Smithsonian agreement in December 1971 provided, at best, an
interim answer to world monetary disorder. The period from September 1972
to June 1974 witnessed an attempt, in the Committee of Twenty, to redesign
the Bretton Woods system, the results of which were embodied in the
Amended IMF Articles finally agreed at the Jamaica meeting of the Interim
Committee in January 1976 and effective from end-March 1978. Compared
with the original aims the reform exercise must be judged a failure: the
authority of the IMF has not been substantially strengthened in several
important areas. The causes of failure clearly illustrate the present-
day constraints under which the IMF must operate.

The Committee of Twenty: composition and aims

Although the events of August 1971 demonstrated the need for
longer term international monetary reform, a consensus was not easily
found either on the forum in which such discussions could take place or
on the terms of reference. The United States was unwilling to use the
Group of Ten framework because it felt isolated from the European participants, a view not unnaturally echoed by developing countries who were not
represented there at all. Moreover, the United States wished the scope
of the reform exercise to include international trade questions, but this
was opposed by EEC countries determined to avoid a possible attack on
their common agricultural policy.

Agreement was finally reached in July 1972 to set up a purpose-
built committee within the framework of the IMF, officially entitled the
Committee of the Board of Governors on Reform of the International
Monetary System and Related Issues. The Committee of Twenty, or C2O as
it was known, was composed of central bank governors and finance ministers
drawn from the twenty constituencies of the IMF Executive Board, in an
attempt to combine decision-making capacity with a representative cross-
section of national viewpoints. As well as nominating one member for the
Committee, each constituency chose two members for the Group of Deputies
in which the detailed work and technical analysis were done. The same
delicate political balance was evident in the choice of Wardhana (Indonesia),
finance minister of a developing country, as Chairman of the Committee and
Morse (United Kingdom) as Chairman of the Deputies. A bureau of four vice-
chairmen, also reasonably representative in terms of geography and doctrine,
was established to co-ordinate the work of the Deputies.

The Committee was given a comprehensive mandate, to advise and
report to the Board of Governors on all aspects of international monetary

21

reform.   In the words of Morse, as reported in the IMF Survey of 17 June 1974, 'we set out in September 1972 to build, as at Bretton Woods, a complete design for an international monetary system that would last for twenty-five years'.

The work of the Committee of Twenty

Between September 1972 and June 1974 the Committee met on six occasions and the Deputies on twelve.   The more specialised aspects of reform were considered in detail by seven advisory technical groups established by the Deputies.   The results of the Committee's work were set out in the June 1974 Outline of Reform which provided a broad framework for a reformed international monetary system.   Its main features, some of which were anticipated in the mid-1972 report on reform by the IMF Executive Directors, can be considered under five headings — adjustment, exchange rates, convertibility, reserve assets and the transfer of real resources to the LDCs.

(a) Adjustment

The Committee recognised the need for symmetry of adjustment responsibilities between reserve centres (principally the United States) and other countries and between surplus and deficit countries, but the relevant part of the Outline was drawn up only in general terms.   It was suggested that a reformed international monetary system should rely on improved consultations within the IMF and on the use of objective indicators which would show when adjustment was necessary.   Members would undertake to implement 'prompt and adequate' adjustment action to correct imbalances, but would be free to decide on its form.   IMF surveillance would be carried out by the Council and the Executive Board, which would assess particular cases of imbalance in the light of the international economic situation.   Where appropriate the Fund could call on a member to adjust and could reinforce that call, in extreme cases, with graduated pressures.

However, agreement could not be reached on a system of indicators to depict what constituted 'imbalance', or on a set of pressures to be used against an offending member.   In the former case, the technical groups concerned could not resolve the form of an indicator system, i.e. whether it should be based on the level of international reserves, as proposed by the United States, on the basic balance of payments, as suggested by the EEC, or on some other cost/price indicator.   Moreover, the technical problems relating to the comparability and availability of the relevant economic data in individual countries were a further area of controversy. A compromise formula, the 'marginal net reserves' approach, was in fact devised by the technical group on adjustment to avoid the problems of basing an indicator system on gross or net reserves.

In theory the starting point for member countries (the 'reserve norm') would be determined on a gross basis and reserve changes thereafter calculated net: but it was not possible to agree on the method of calculating initial reserve norms — whether at one point in time or as determined by one of several possible formulae — or on the extent of permissible movements in reserves before IMF pressures would be activated to compel adjustment.   An additional stumbling block was the proposed treatment of countries' eurocurrency liabilities and the external

positions of commercial banks. If included within the definition of
reserves these would have added considerably to the administrative
burden of monitoring a reserve indicator system; if excluded, any such
system would have been an unrealistic starting point for the intended
clarification of adjustment responsibilities.

It also proved easier to list a set of pressures or sanctions
against countries in imbalance than to agree on how they should be
employed. The types of suggested pressures were wide-ranging. For
surplus countries they included the loss of future SDR allocations,
levies on the accumulation of excess reserves and the depositing of
excess reserves with the IMF at a negative interest rate. For deficit
countries they incorporated graduated charges on IMF drawings, levies on
reserve deficiencies and strict limits on official international borrowing. However, there was no consensus of opinion on whether the activation of these pressures should be at the IMF's discretion or presumptive
(that is, automatic).

(b) The exchange rate mechanism

The C20 suggested that the reformed international monetary system
should be based on 'stable but adjustable par values' with provision for
floating exchange rates in 'particular situations' subject to IMF authorisation. Members would be required to maintain 'specified maximum
exchange rate margins' for their currencies, which could be varied for
all countries by a special majority in the IMF Executive Board. A more
symmetrical system of exchange market intervention than that prevalent
before 1971 should be established, involving intervention in SDRs or in
a selected group of some ten to twenty major currencies and not solely in
US dollars. In this way equivalent margins could be operative for all
currencies, including the dollar, which, it was hoped, would allow the
United States greater freedom in its exchange rate policy.

These proposals were already anachronistic in mid-1974. The oil
crisis postponed for a considerable time any chance of a widespread return
to par values and, with the continuation of floating, the direct relevance
of introducing a symmetrical intervention system has disappeared. Each
country now 'manages' its own exchange rate in the light of national
economic interests, and exchange market intervention does not revolve
around stable parities, as is examined more fully in Chapter Six. Even
if a return to par values could have been implemented no recommendation
was made as to which of the two symmetric intervention systems, SDR or
multi-currency, should be adopted: and neither were there any effective
proposals for protecting par values against the increasing likelihood of
large unpredictable capital flows. In this latter context the C20 merely
hoped that improved consultation in the IMF would produce co-ordinated
actions to limit 'disequilibrating' movements.

In an important sense the C20's endorsement of stable but adjustable par values, which owed as much to the lack of a generally accepted
alternative as to conservative prejudice and the self-interest of
developing countries, undermined other aspects of international monetary
reform. As Williamson has argued (1977) it raised doubts over the
practicability of a reserve indicator system which, combined with such
an exchange rate régime, might have given owners of short-term capital
clear signals of likely parity changes and caused greater instability than
before 1973. It also reduced the chances of putting any sort of coherent

new monetary system into place because of the growing lack of realism of one of its central supports.

On the other hand, the C20 did make an attempt to come to terms with exchange rate developments since mid-1973, in the form of the June 1974 Guidelines for Floating which it was suggested that members should observe. The essence of the Guidelines was that countries should:

(i) smooth out very short-term (daily or weekly) fluctuations in market exchange rates;

(ii) offer some resistance to market tendencies in the slightly longer run (monthly or quarterly) where 'temporary' factors were at work; and

(iii) resist movements in market rates which appeared to be deviating substantially from the appropriate medium-term norm agreed between the member and the IMF.

There was also the suggestion, nothing more, that members' intervention policies should be linked to reserve targets, a proposal which looked back to the unresolved debate on objective indicators. Members were expected, as under Bretton Woods rules, to avoid the imposition of current account restrictions and were specifically enjoined to take account of other members' interests in their intervention strategies. Aggressive intervention in support of market movements to bring about competitive exchange rate alteration was frowned upon, for fear of a return to 1930s' conditions.

The Guidlines were designed as the basis for 'meaningful dialogue' between the IMF and its members with a view to promoting internationally responsible and internationally consistent exchange rate policies. They were an important starting point for IMF surveillance, reaffirming the principle that exchange rates were a matter of international concern, yet allowing considerable freedom in national policy. However, there is little indication that individual countries adhered to them. The proposal for medium-term exchange rate norms or target zones was effectively blocked by the US commitment to flexible rates which can be explained by the relatively small size of the US external sector and the correspondingly high price, in terms of unemployment, of correcting a payments deficit through domestic restrictions. The other provisions were unenforceable, not least because of the absence of a universally agreed and easily measurable concept of an effective (trade-weighted) exchange rate which could be used in IMF surveillance. The Guidelines were not sufficiently precise in themselves to provide countries with guidance in specific situations: and in practice few countries have been able to afford the luxury of a coherent medium-term intervention strategy. More usually the policy since 1973 has been one of resisting rapid rate movements, followed by an attempt to assess whether the pressure indicated underlying disequilibrium and longer-term trends.

(c) Convertibility, consolidation and management of reserves

The C20 clearly outlined the objectives in these areas but achieved little else. It was hoped that there would be symmetrical obligations on all countries (including the United States), better management of global liquidity, adequate elasticity (time to pay) and reasonable freedom for countries to choose the composition of their own reserves. That

these aims were not realised was due largely to disagreement between the
United States and the EEC over a reformed settlement system.   The EEC
advocated a 'more mandatory' system which would have required a 'settlement group' of major countries to carry out, under IMF supervision,
immediate settlement of imbalances in primary reserve assets.   In effect
the deficits and surpluses of all countries would be reflected in a loss
or gain of reserve assets rather than, as in the case of the United States,
sometimes being financed by issuing reserve liabilities.   Asset-settlement,
as it was called, would have ensured that the United States was subject to
the same (reserve) pressures to adjust as any other country — a necessary
condition for collective international control over the volume of official
reserves through SDR allocations and cancellations.

The United States, on the other hand, was only prepared to accept
a more limited 'on demand' settlement system which would have preserved an
important reserve currency role for the dollar with attendant advantages
such as the ability to avoid costly adjustment measures and freedom from
foreign financial constraints.   The US proposals envisaged a restoration
of dollar convertibility into primary reserve assets (SDRs), but only when
the US liquidity position was judged sufficiently strong and even then
subject to strict country limits, established with reference to the
proposed reserve indicator system described above.   This fundamental
difference of view reflected the very different US and European interpret-
ations of the breakdown of the Bretton Woods system.   When combined with
US opposition to controls on reserve currency holdings and LDC insistence
on freedom to deposit reserves in the eurocurrency markets, it became
almost impossible for the C20 to devise 'appropriate arrangements' for
supervising official currency balances in the future.

The position of existing reserve currency holdings, the so-called
dollar 'overhang', was also left undecided.   The Outline mentioned the
possible consolidation of such balances over time, but not how this was
to be achieved, whether through bilateral funding or a Substitution
Account within the IMF.   The problem of elasticity — that is, the
ability to finance current and capital account disequilibria — was similarly deferred with vague references to bilateral, regional and IMF
credit facilities.

(d) Primary reserve assets

The Outline of Reform stated categorically that the SDR would
become the principal reserve asset of a reformed international monetary
system and that the role of gold and of reserve currencies would be
reduced.   However, as already shown, the C20 was unable to agree on
measures to phase out the reserve currency role of the US dollar and
there was similar disagreement on the future of monetary gold.   On the
one hand it was generally accepted that the limited supply, speculative
price changes and uneven country distribution of monetary gold made it
unsuitable as a reserve asset: on the other hand the C20 recognised that
gold reserves were an important component of global liquidity, which
should be usable to finance balance of payments deficits.   Three possible
ways of achieving this last aim were mentioned in the Outline but nothing
substantive was decided.

Partial agreement on gold was eventually reached by the Interim
Committee in August 1975, the main features of which have been incorporated into the Amended Articles.   They include elimination of gold's

function as common denominator of a restored par value system, abolition of the old official price, freedom to adopt national gold policies so long as these avoid maintenance of a fixed price and the ending of obligatory gold payments by members to the IMF. In addition the Fund has been authorised to dispose of 50 million ounces of its own gold, acquired through members' subscription payments, with the possibility of selling the remaining 100 million ounces at the old official price or on the free market.

These changes, which are analysed in more detail in Chapters Six and Seven, disguise continuing fundamental differences of opinion, and future IMF gold operations will be subject to high voting majorities. A new element of uncertainty was introduced in early 1978 by the ending of the two-year agreement of February 1976 involving the Group of Ten countries and Switzerland to limit their aggregate gold reserves and to take no action to peg the price of gold. The position of gold as a reserve asset, therefore, remains ambiguous.

Moreover the C20 did little to enhance the status of the SDR, except in one important respect — the method of valuation. Before the reform exercise the IMF Articles specified that SDR 1 was equivalent to 0.888671 grammes of fine gold, which corresponded in 1969 to the par value of the dollar, so that SDR 1 equalled US$1. Exchange rates for other currencies against the SDR were calculated from the market exchange rates for these currencies against the dollar in accordance with the equal value principle. During a period of fixed exchange rates, the value of the SDR tended to be stable in transactions against individual currencies and so against currencies in general: except when par values changed, it fluctuated only to the extent of the permitted exchange margin between a particular currency and the US dollar. A change in par value affected the value of the SDR against the currency concerned: and over time the SDR's value could change against currencies generally, the size and direction of the change depending on the balance between devaluations and revaluations.

The suspension of dollar convertibility, the adoption of wider margins and two formal devaluations of the US dollar led to substantially wider fluctuations in the transactions value of the SDR against currencies other than the dollar, a volatility which conflicted with the aim of making the SDR the principal reserve asset. Widespread floating made it irrational to continue with a fixed link between one currency (the dollar) and the SDR and, in July 1974, a new method of valuation was introduced, designed to ensure a stable value for the SDR against currencies in general.

The new method, known as the 'standard basket', was adopted for an interim period only, without prejudice to the method of valuation to be used under a reformed system. Three alternative approaches — the 'asymmetrical', 'adjustable' and 'par value' methods — were rejected as unworkable in a régime of floating exchange rates. According to Williamson (1977) the standard basket was the only one which provided 'an unambiguous consistent valuation of the SDR no matter what happened to the exchange rate régime and went furthest in insulating the SDR's purchasing power from capricious variation over time'.

Under the standard basket one SDR was equal to the sum of specified quantities of the sixteen currencies whose issuers each accounted for more than 1% of world exports of goods and services in the period 1968-72:

Units of currency in one SDR

US dollar	0.40	Belgian franc	1.6
Deutschemark	0.38	Swedish krona	0.13
Sterling	0.C45	Australian dollar	0.C12
French franc	0.44	Danish krone	0.11
Japanese yen	26	Norwegian krone	0.099
Canadian dollar	0.071	Spanish peseta	1.1
Italian lira	47	Austrian schilling	0.22
Netherlands guilder	0.14	South African rand	0.0082

Source: *Bank of England Quarterly Bulletin*, September 1974

The weightings used to determine the quantities of each currency were based mainly on exports (adjusted, particularly in the case of the United States, for special factors) as follows:

Weights used to determine the basket (%)

United States	33	Belgium	3.5
West Germany	12.5	Sweden	2.5
United Kingdom	9	Australia	1.5
France	7.5	Denmark	1.5
Japan	7.5	Norway	1.5
Canada	6	Spain	1.5
Italy	6	Austria	1
Netherlands	4.5	South Africa	1

Source: *Bank of England Quarterly Bulletin*, September 1974

The calculations ensured that there was no discontinuity in the SDR's value. On 28 June 1974 SDR 1 equalled US$1.20635, the same as under the old method, but it has since fluctuated freely in line with market rates. The value of the SDR is calculated daily by the Fund in terms not only of the sixteen reference currencies but of each currency used in SDR transactions and in IMF drawings. The exchange rates used are supplied under standing arrangements by the authorities in major exchange markets.

The availability of these rates, which are regularly published, has contributed, along with its comparative stability and wide geographical coverage, to the extension of the SDR's role as an international unit of account. Its adoption by the IMF in 1972 was followed by the successful placement of three SDR-denominated euromarket issues in 1975 and by the denomination of Suez canal tolls in SDRs. The International Air Transport Association now uses it as the central reference unit for negotiating world passenger fares and cargo rates and there has been periodic talk of the SDR replacing the dollar as denominator of OPEC oil prices. If this happened the Arab example could influence other international commodity groups.

Continued exchange market instability and the limited impact of other more complicated currency cocktails would seem to augur well for a continuation of this role in the medium term. However, the momentum has slowed since 1975-76 and the OPEC countries are clearly reluctant to abandon the dollar despite its large depreciation between mid-1977 and mid-1978. The method of valuation has been left open in the Amended Articles which could be a source of uncertainty among potential users even though, while floating continues, any change is likely to be relatively minor. The only change so far has been the inclusion (with effect from July 1978) of the Saudi Arabian and Iranian currencies in the SDR valuation basket, at the expense of the South African rand and the Danish krone, together with an adjustment of the individual currency weightings.

The Outline of Reform also stated that the effective yield on the SDR should be high enough to make it attractive to acquire and hold, but not so high as to make countries reluctant to use the SDR when in deficit. To this end the interest rate on the SDR was raised from 1½% to 5% in July 1974 and was made subject, from January 1975 onwards, to a formula relating it to a weighted average of daily market interest rates on short-term obligations in five main centres, as follows:

	Weights %
United States: yields for three-month Treasury bills	47
West Germany: three-month inter-bank deposits	18
United Kingdom: yields for three-month Treasury bills	13
France: three-month inter-bank rate against private paper	11
Japan: call money market rate (unconditional)	11
	100

Source: *Bank of England Quarterly Bulletin*, September 1974

Unless the Executive Board decides otherwise, the SDR interest rate changes if the above average falls below 9% or rises above 11%. When this happens the SDR rate, starting at 5%, is adjusted by three-fifths of the movement in the average rate beyond 9% or 11%, the result being rounded to the nearest ¼%.

The formula was a compromise between IMF debtors, who have to pay interest on their net use of SDRs, and creditors, who earn interest at the same rate on SDRs held in excess of their allocations. It reflected not only the SDR's inherent 'security discount' and the general desire for comparability rather than equality with currency assets, but also the opposition of developing countries, as debtors, to a more realistic level. The interest rate is subject to a 70% majority in the Amended Articles and remains a very sensitive and controversial issue.

As well as the method of valuation and the interest rate, the C20 made several recommendations for modifying the SDR's characteristics and relaxing the constraints on its use which were outlined in Chapter Two. Many of these have been incorporated into the Amended Articles. Participants will be able to enter into transactions by agreement without IMF authorisation and such transactions need not observe the requirement of need. The IMF may now authorise 'operations' in SDRs between participants that are not otherwise provided for in the Articles, subject to appropriate safeguards. The Fund will also be able to broaden the categories of official holders of SDRs and the range of transactions in which they may

engage.   In addition the SDR will be usable in more IMF operations,
notably in payment of quota increases, sales to members for currencies
of other members, members' purchases, and distribution of IMF income
(Amended Articles XV-XXV).

        However, the proposed changes will only create the potential for
greater use of SDRs.   The widening of permissible operations in SDRs
will be subject to high voting majorities and such operations will, as
now, be confined to official entities.   The stipulation of a minimum
balance (reconstitution) will remain, although these provisions may be
changed or abrogated by a lower voting majority, and designation will
continue to be the only way participants may be certain of obtaining
currency in exchange for SDRs.

        More generally, the principles governing the allocation and
cancellation of SDRs will not be changed in the new Articles despite LDC
pressure for some relaxation (mentioned in Annex 8 of the C20's Outline of
Reform). No substantive progress has been made, before or after June
1974, towards the substitution of SDRs for gold and reserve currencies.
The C20 was unable to resolve the various technical and political problems and the idea of an SDR substitution facility within the IMF was
forgotten until early 1978. (This is examined in Chapter Six.)   The
less radical idea, proposed by Witteveen in early 1975, for countries to
hold a minimum percentage of their reserves in SDRs was also a non-starter.
Even this scheme, designed to secure a measure of international control
over official reserves without a drastic reduction in the role of reserve
currencies, was too much for the United States.   At best its effect would
have been marginal: it would have been difficult to enforce and would
probably have been unworkable given the recent instability in international
payments.

        In sum the C20 and its successor the Interim Committee have merely
tinkered with the SDR.   The Amended Article VII includes only a vague
provision to the effect that members should collaborate in order to ensure
better international surveillance of international liquidity and the development of the SDR as the principal reserve asset.   This is meaningless in
the absence of collectively agreed obligations collectively enforced and
it is totally unrealistic in the context of the vast expansion in private
(commercial bank) financing of payments deficits since 1973.   The
increased availability of private credit, notably through the euromarkets,
has immeasurably complicated the task of managing global liquidity and
the question has been virtually shelved, with the result that the SDR has
been relegated to a minor form of international credit.

(e) Transfer of real resources to LDCs

        Although the June 1974 Outline stressed the importance of adequate
arrangements to promote real resource flows to LDCs for economic development, it contained only one definite proposal — the establishment of an
extended fund facility, which is examined in Chapter Six.   A number of
other measures were taken in 1974, notably the setting up of an oil
facility and a joint IMF-IBRD Development Committee, but they were more
related to the oil crisis than to the transfer of real resources in the
longer-term context of international monetary reform.

        The question of establishing a link between development assistance
and SDR allocations was thoroughly explored by the C20 but neither the

principle nor the form could be agreed. In essence the principles governing the total volume of SDR allocations would have been unchanged, but the formula for the distribution of allocations would have been amended to give developing countries a larger share than they would otherwise have received on the basis of their share in IMF quotas. Linked resources so allocated would then have been distributed to all developing countries according to development needs and in such a way as to be relatively favourable to the least developed countries.

For many countries, not just LDCs, the reform exercise was seen as an opportunity to bring about a modest improvement in the distribution of world income through the relatively new SDR facility. The advocates of a link argued that it would constitute a net addition to aid flows and would improve the average quality of such flows, particularly if linked resources were not tied to expenditure in any one country. The link would assist economic development directly, via the provision of financial resources, and indirectly, through the encouragement of trade, thereby contributing to a smoother adjustment process. In no way was it envisaged that the link would prejudice the SDR's primary function as a reserve asset.

Against this it was contended that a link would unnecessarily complicate the international monetary system and provoke offsetting reductions in other aid flows. Confidence in the SDR would be undermined if it were to be backed by an unduly large proportion of high risk developing country obligations. The link would also be inflationary since it might involve 'excessive' allocations of SDRs related to 'infinite' development needs. Most importantly, development aid and international liquidity creation were seen as separate issues only incidentally related, each with its own economics and its own politics. As Williamson (1973) has shown, the idea that the Fund might become more of a development agency was strongly opposed by important creditors such as West Germany and the United States, who also pointed to the potential problems of reducing the volume of international liquidity if the cancellation of SDRs were to involve calling in loans to developing countries.

Apart from these ideological differences, no decision was reached on important technical matters such as the timing of linked allocations, the amounts involved, the distribution of linked resources among recipients and the criteria for use. Three possible forms of a link were inconclusively examined — direct allocations of SDRs to developing countries, direct allocations to international and regional development finance institutions for disbursement to LDCs and voluntary transfers by developed countries of part of their SDR allocations to development institutions. Not surprisingly LDCs favoured the first approach, many developed countries the third. None would have been without difficulties as regards equitable distribution, effective use and maintenance of confidence in the SDR as a reserve asset. Even assuming agreement on a further allocation of SDRs in the near future — a possibility which is considered more fully in Chapter Seven — the prospects for the link would appear very slight.

The implications of failure

Several reasons have been advanced for the disappointing results achieved by the C20. The official explanation centred on the unsettled state of the world economy and it has been argued that unprecedented levels of world inflation and the dramatic rise in oil prices in 1973-74 made impossible the introduction of a coherent new system.   Certainly the shock of these disturbances made countries less willing to accept new commitments even though the need for an agreed adjustment framework was that much greater than before.

More serious from the point of view of present day problems was the lack of sufficient political will on the part of several countries. The position of the developing countries has been described by Williamson (1977) as 'all asking, no bargaining' and this was particularly true with regard to claims for special treatment in any system of reserve indicators and in any limitations on placing reserves in euromarket deposits yielding high rates of interest.   A similar reluctance to compromise was shown by the United States, which refused to accept any real diminution in the dollar's central role or to countenance an SDR/aid link.   After the Smithsonian agreement the United States had very little to gain from reform, which lends truth to the observation by Kafka (1976), then an Executive Director of the IMF, that the real reason why no more was accomplished was simply that no compelling need was felt for anything more.

The lack of political will was compounded by technical failings on the part of the C20 which have been examined in some detail by 'inside' commentators such as Williamson (1977) and Crockett (1977).   Perhaps the main one was the unwillingness to negotiate in the technical groups — the Deputies spent much time listening to prepared statements of national positions — which was heightened by the relatively passive role of the C20's bureau (international secretariat).   Of equal importance was the C20's failure of vision in crucial areas, not least the endorsement of an exchange rate régime which was no longer viable and the failure to devise arrangements to deal with destabilising private capital flows.

In short the reform exercise demonstrated the narrow limits of international monetary co-operation.   In comparison with the structured system devised at Bretton Woods the Amended Articles provide only indistinct ground rules for members' policies.   According to Williamson (1976) the world is to function on the basis of a set of conventions and practices that have evolved 'out of a mixture of custom and crisis'.

CHAPTER FOUR

INTERNATIONAL ADJUSTMENT SINCE 1973

The failure of international monetary reform has deprived the IMF of an effective framework within which to supervise international adjustment. The IMF's influence has also been seriously challenged by the unprecedented economic developments since 1973, including sharp changes in the prices of many commodities, enormous balance of payments disturbances, major inflation and serious recession. As yet the IMF has played only a minor role in handling these problems, partly because of its limited financial resources — analysed in Chapters Six and Seven — but mainly because of the reluctance of governments to accept constraints on policy-making.

This chapter examines the nature and distribution of the present and prospective imbalance in international payments, an imbalance which is unprecedented in size. The combined current account surplus of OPEC countries summed over the three years 1974 to 1976 was $142 billion. In the same period the combined surplus of the United States, West Germany, Japan, Switzerland and the Benelux countries totalled $38 billion. Among the deficit groups France, the United Kingdom, Italy and Canada shared a deficit of $50 billion between them, and the other OECD countries also ran an aggregate deficit of $50 billion. The non-oil developing countries recorded a deficit of $78 billion.

Within the overall pattern of imbalance several distinct but inter-related strands can be identified. The principal elements are, in the broadest sense, 'structural' and therefore medium to long term. These include the oil deficits resulting from the 1973-74 price increases, which can only be reduced by comprehensive energy strategies and large-scale expansion of exports to the oil-producers; the persistent deficits of developing countries, most of which must import essential goods and services for development; and the chronic surpluses of countries such as West Germany and Japan which have traditionally relied on export-led growth. Of equal importance is the emergence of a substantial current account deficit in the United States which has far-reaching implications for the international economy. In all cases appropriate domestic policy measures will take time to have a lasting effect.

The oil surplus

The continuing OPEC surplus remains one of the major preoccupations of international financial authorities and markets. After initial fears that the surplus would prove unmanageable, the aggregate annual total was halved to $35 billion in 1975 as a result of the rapid expansion in OPEC

imports and reduced world demand for OPEC oil.   In 1976 the surplus rose
again due to several unexpected factors including a slowdown in OPEC import
growth, improved OPEC terms of trade and delays in developing alternative
energy sources by industrial countries; but it fell to $33 billion in 1977.

        The outlook to 1982 depends on three uncertain variables — world
demand for OPEC oil, the price of OPEC oil and the import capacity of OPEC
countries, particularly the hard core surplus countries of the Arabian pen-
insula.   Private sector forecasts are optimistic.   According to de Vries
(1977), vice-president of Morgan Guaranty, the OPEC surplus is likely to
be pared to $10 billion by 1980, becoming more moderate and manageable
each year.   After 1980, OPEC oil exports may rise as other sources
decline, but the surplus is expected to remain around $10 billion even if
President Carter's 1977 energy proposals are only partially implemented.
This view relies crucially on a high rate of import absorption by Kuwait,
the UAE, Qatar and Saudi Arabia, particularly the last-named which will
have a 'pivotal role' in the future course of the OPEC surplus and in
international adjustment generally.   On similar assumptions Citibank
(July 1977) also expects the OPEC surplus to fall — to $17 billion by
1980 — in response to enhanced economic opportunities in the OPEC countries.

        Official forecasts are less encouraging in view of the 1977 oil
price increases and the assumption of rising world demand in 1978-79,
insufficient conservation and slower OPEC import absorption.   Burns
(April 1977), then chairman of the Federal Reserve Board of Governors,
argued that the surplus was eroding 'slowly if at all' and Witteveen
(May 1977), speaking as IMF Managing Director, forecast only 'some reduction' over the next few years at a fairly gradual rate.   This does not
mean that the surplus will present an insuperable problem.   Indeed it is
declining more rapidly than would have been thought possible four years
ago and, as the IMF staff pointed out in May 1977, the estimated 1977
surplus was approximately equivalent to the combined current account
surplus of the industrial countries between 1967 and 1972 (rescaled to
1977 price and output levels).   However, it is generally accepted that
the OPEC surplus, and the counterpart deficits in the rest of the world,
will be a feature of international payments for some time to come.   This
will inevitably involve OPEC customers in continuing large-scale financing
operations even assuming all reasonable speed in adjustment on their part.

The oil deficits

        A second major problem, made more urgent by the 1976 upward move-
ment in the OPEC surplus, concerns the distribution of deficits among the
oil-importing countries.   The problem is not due exclusively to higher oil
prices as the following analysis by Burns in April 1977 makes clear:

        'The payments deficits of various nations, both industrial and
        less developed, can be traced to extensive social welfare and
        development programmes undertaken in the early '70s and financed
        by heavy government borrowing, often directly from central banks.
        Even when the internal stresses resulting from inflation were
        aggravated by the oil burden and by weaker exports, there was
        little or no adjustment of economic policies in numerous instances,
        thus causing external positions to deteriorate sharply'.

There have been notable exceptions to this pattern, particularly countries such as West Germany and Japan, historically sensitive to inflation or payments imbalance. The resultant diversity within the non-OPEC sector has been accentuated by the varying impact of the 1974-75 recession and by differing recovery trends.

(a) Developed countries

According to the IMF staff in May 1977, the aggregate current account position of industrial countries, defined as the Group of Ten plus Austria, Norway and Switzerland, worsened from an average annual surplus of $10.2 billion between 1967 and 1972 to an estimated near balance in 1977. In the wider group of OECD countries the most striking developments in 1976-77 were the emergence of a substantial deficit in the United States and a tripling of the Japanese surplus. West Germany and Switzerland remained in surplus and, although there was a marked improvement in the current account position of France, Italy and the United Kingdom, the external position of smaller OECD countries such as Portugal and Turkey if anything worsened after 1974-75.

According to the OECD Secretariat (December 1977) the prospects were hardly reassuring for the next few years. On the basis of a 1978-79 average growth rate of $3\frac{1}{2}$%-4%, well below the $5\frac{1}{4}$% annual target for the period 1975-80 agreed by OECD finance ministers in mid-1976, unemployment for the OECD as a whole was predicted to rise to over $5\frac{1}{4}$% of the labour force. In 1978 export volumes were expected to grow faster than import volumes and the aggregate OECD current deficit might be reduced from $32 billion in 1977 to around $20 billion. But, although the United Kingdom, Italy and France could strengthen their positions in 1978-79, most of the present imbalances were thought likely to persist with the United States deficit widening to nearly $25 billion (in 1978), those of the smaller OECD countries remaining very large and the surpluses of Japan and West Germany being roughly unchanged or higher. There was general agreement that imbalances of this magnitude might not be sustainable in the medium term without damaging the present trade and payments system.

The size of the US trade deficit and the depreciation of the dollar against other major currencies between mid-1977 and mid-1978 have raised important questions in international finance. The US current account (trade plus invisibles) deteriorated from a surplus of $11.6 billion in 1975 to near balance in 1976 and record deficit ($20.2 billion) in 1977. The latter figure represented about $1\frac{1}{2}$% of GNP, not substantially less than the current deficits of other industrial countries since 1972, which in their cases necessitated corrective action. As Morgan Guaranty (September 1977) pointed out, the 1977 deficit was far larger than could be justified with reference to the US economy's 'locomotive' role in stimulating world growth.

The deterioration has been concentrated on the trade side. In 1977 the trade deficit totalled $34.1 billion and no improvement is expected by the US Administration before 1979. The negative swing after 1975 was due to four main factors — the disparity between the growth rates of the United States and other major countries, the failure to curb US oil imports, rapid industrialisation among developing countries and a turn-round in US agricultural trade. In the first instance, the United States was (in 1978) the only major country where the post-1975 recovery

was well established.   Real GNP rose by 4.9% in 1977, compared with 2½%
in West Germany, and growth is officially forecast at 4-5% in 1978 and
1979 with the aid of tax cuts worth $20 billion in early 1979.   Not only
has the United States led the world recovery, but the pattern of US
consumer-led growth and weak investment abroad also added to the deficit,
since capital goods weigh heavily in US exports while consumer goods dom-
inate imports.   The depreciation of the dollar against the other major
currencies between mid-1977 and mid-1978 should help to boost US exports
to West Germany and Japan in 1978-80, but the benefits could be partially
offset by slower US productivity gains and a relative increase in the US
rate of inflation.   A possible reduction of the US deficit through the
pursuit of more expansionary policies by West Germany and Japan has been
the subject of acrimonious public dispute since mid-1977.

         The second major factor behind the increasing US trade deficit
has been the downward trend of domestic energy supplies during the 1970s,
combined with the quadrupling of OPEC oil prices at end-1973.   In 1977
the oil import bill was an estimated $42 billion, compared with only $3
billion in 1970, and, with little public response to conservation efforts
and no chance of energy legislation being effective in the short run, no
improvement is expected by the Administration before 1979.   Further
deterioration could occur over this period if there is any increase in
the price of OPEC oil to compensate for the decline in real OPEC revenues
caused by the depreciation of the dollar.

         There is evident scope for an effective US energy policy which
could, in the medium term, reduce both the domestic current account deficit
and the surplus of the OPEC countries.   The prospects are not encouraging.
Even the full rigours of Carter's 1977 plan, designed to reduce growth in
energy demand from 5% to 2% in 1985 and cut oil imports by some four
million barrels per day, would not, by most estimates, have had much
impact on the overall situation.   Moreover the original proposals have
been considerably amended by Congress and the eventual legislation will
certainly fall well short of a final solution to US energy problems and
may have to be only the first in a series of energy bills.

         Apart from the deficit with other OECD and with OPEC countries,
US manufacturing trade has been adversely affected by rapid industrialisation in a sizeable number of lower-wage LDCs in Asia and Latin America.
This has led to a shift in production of a growing volume of products away
from the United States and thus to greater competition in US export markets.
At the same time traditional US customers, notably Brazil and Mexico,
successfully cut their imports in 1976-78 as part of comprehensive stabil-
isation programmes to reduce their balance of payments deficits.   A US
Treasury estimate attributed over one-sixth of the trade deterioration in
the first half of 1977 to Brazil and Mexico alone.   The signs are that
LDC import growth in 1978-80 will not lead to any significant increase in
US exports.

         Finally US agricultural exports, historically a major growth sector,
were depressed in 1977 by buoyant world harvests.   A notable exception to
the trend of falling commodity prices was coffee,which accounted for a large
part of the rise in agricultural imports in the first half of the year.
Despite the possibility of large sales of grain to the USSR, the agricultural sector is unlikely to improve sufficiently to have any real impact on
the trade deficit before 1979 at the earliest.

         The large size of the US trade deficit, present and prospective,

was one reason for the weakness of the dollar against other major currencies between September 1977 and April 1978,but it was not the only one.
The substantial depreciation stemmed as much from lack of confidence in
the Carter Administration's economic policies, particularly as regards
inflation and energy legislation, and from long-term currency diversification of the portfolios of international corporations, banks and other
financial institutions.   Lack of confidence in the present Administration was perhaps hardly surprising given the absence of a coherent
dollar strategy.   In 1977 the US authorities intermittently tried to
'talk the dollar down' with apparent disregard for the disruptive effects
of sudden exchange rate shifts on the economies of its major trading
partners.   In early 1978 the policy of 'malign neglect' (as it is known
in Europe) was replaced by more active intervention to 'check speculation
and restore order' in the foreign exchange markets.   The change was
signalled in the form of two agreements between the US and West German
authorities, in January and March respectively, designed to provide the
US government with sufficient resources to support the dollar and counter
'disorderly conditions'.

However, intervention is at best a short-term response, as the
United Kingdom has discovered in the past, and cannot alter the factors
underlying the dollar's weakness.   In this respect the US-West German
agreements did not mention any new policy initiatives by either government to improve the US current balance nor any measures to deal with the
large shift out of dollar assets by international investors since the
fourth quarter of 1977.   Some diversification would probably have taken
place, irrespective of the US current account weakness, as part of a
longer-term adjustment of the currency mix of international portfolios
to take account of the decline in US economic power relative to countries
such as West Germany and Japan.   The problem is that some 80% of eurocurrency deposits and a similar proportion of official reserves are in
dollars, so that even very small movements out of dollars have a disproportionate effect on exchange rates.   The moves towards diversification
contributed to the unsettled monetary and trading conditions in the mid-
1977 - mid-1978 period and revived the C20 debate on the outstanding
dollar balances, which is examined more fully in Chapter Six.

Together with the United States and Japan, West Germany is now
widely regarded as one of the three 'locomotives' of the world economy.
Apart from being the largest European economy, West Germany is the world's
second largest trading country with the largest official reserves and one
of the lowest inflation rates.

However, since early 1977 there have been growing doubts in the
rest of the world over whether West Germany is fulfilling her international obligations.   After real growth of 5¾% in 1976 the economic
recovery faltered: real GNP rose by only 2½% in 1977 and the most optimistic official forecast was 3½% for 1978.   In contrast the 1977 trade
surplus of $16.6 billion was the second highest on record and the current
account surplus was slightly up from its 1976 level of $3.4 billion.   It
seems possible that the current surplus will rise again in 1978-80
assuming, *inter alia*, a much slower outflow of dividend payments than in
1977.

The West German reluctance to reflate to help other countries is
now proverbial.   The authorities argue that the scope for further stimulation is restricted by fears of inflation, the traditionally high savings
ratio — which would reduce the effectiveness of tax cuts to boost

consumption — and the constitutional ban on Federal Government borrowing to finance current (as opposed to investment) expenditure.   They point also to the historically low level of West German interest rates and to relatively expansionary money supply targets — 8% in 1978, for example, which was broadly in line with the expected rise in nominal GNP.   Further-more the budget for 1978 was somewhat more stimulatory than its 1976 and 1977 predecessors (when the public sector financial deficit contracted by $6.5 billion and $2.5 billion respectively):   tax cuts for industry and consumers were combined with plans to speed up medium-term infra-structural investment.

On the other hand, the effectiveness of the German measures is open to question.   The repercussions of earlier fiscal restraint may still be felt in the 1978-80 period, particularly in view of the reluc-tance of the regional authorities (Länder) to increase their outlays, which account for roughly half of public sector spending.   Secondly, the curtailment of the nuclear energy programme in 1978 will have an adverse impact on public investment well into the 1980s.   Business sur-veys in the first half of 1978 showed little optimism among manufacturers, with reports of patchy capital investment and low levels of capacity util-isation, especially in the basic industries (iron, steel, chemicals) most affected by the 1977-78 appreciation of the Deutschemark.

Prima facie there would seem to be a strong case for further stimulation over the medium term.   There may be room for the creation of more energy-related investment projects and, more importantly for world trade, for tax cuts aimed particularly at the lower paid whose average propensity to save may be lower than other groups.   These might be com-bined with measures to reduce the attractiveness of saving and increase expenditure on consumer goods which have a high import content.   The greater stimulus might lead to bottlenecks in certain sectors but would be unlikely to have much effect on inflation given the large margin of spare capacity (in mid-1978) throughout much of industry.

Similar complaints have been voiced against Japan.   The economic recovery here was also precarious in mid-1978 and real growth in the year ending March 1978 was well below the government's original 6.7% target. What growth there was was essentially due to substantial increases in government expenditure and exports: in calendar 1977 the trade surplus was a record $17.6 billion and the current surplus $11.1 billion after initial government forecasts of a small deficit.

For the year to March 1979 the authorities set a 7% real growth target and introduced a moderately stimulatory budget.   Their growth strategy relied heavily on a further large rise in public expenditure intended to boost private consumption and imports.   The external surplus was initially expected to narrow to $13.5 billion on trade and $6.0 billion on current account (although the government did not hold these as definite targets).   But the chances of achieving these aims are slight. A similar strategy failed in 1977 and the outlook (in mid-1978) for private and particularly business spending is doubtful over the period to 1980.   Private forecasters put real growth at only 4½-5½% in fiscal 1978 which would make it impossible to reduce the current surplus to less than $8½-9 billion.

As in West Germany there would seem to be scope for further stimulation, particularly since inflation was running at a very low annual rate in the first half of 1978.   Although the authorities took a number

of positive steps in mid-1978, including interest rate cuts and proposals
to stockpile raw materials and purchase foreign aircraft, they are unlikely
to have any real impact on the huge external surplus.   While further
supplementary budgets cannot be ruled out in 1978-79, the policy of piecemeal concessions to international opinion will probably remain unchanged
in the medium term.

(b) Advanced primary producers

The outlook for these countries as a group (defined by the IMF as
Australia, New Zealand, South Africa, Finland, Greece, Iceland, Ireland,
Malta, Portugal, Romania, Spain, Turkey and Yugoslavia) is far from
encouraging, as the February 1978 Scandinavian currency fluctuations bear
witness.   Real economic growth rates averaged only 3% in 1976 and are not
expected to recover much until 1979.   Price increases continue at a high
level and, as the IMF staff has shown (May 1977), the estimated $12-13
billion aggregate current account deficit in 1977 was twice the size of
the 1967-72 average in real terms.   Any improvement in the aggregate
current balance since 1974 has been in the non-European members of this
group, which were the first to adopt stabilisation programmes.   In contrast political problems have impaired the ability and willingness of
countries such as Portugal and Turkey to adopt the necessary restrictive
policies.

(c) Developing countries

For most non-oil developing countries the situation has deteriorated markedly since 1973, when, as Costanzo (1975), vice-chairman of
Citibank, has shown, many experienced record increases in export volumes,
export prices and foreign exchange reserves.   The group was then hit in
quick succession by the rise in oil prices, recession in industrial
countries, the collapse of commodity prices and high world inflation.
In general the LDCs have had less scope for curbing oil consumption than
industrial countries and they have not been in a position to expand their
exports significantly to OPEC.   Their exports have also suffered from the
relative slack in world demand since 1974-75 and, more recently, from the
imposition of protectionist measures in industrial countries.

In 1974 and 1975 the average ratio of LDC reserves to imports fell
to 25% and 23% respectively, considerably lower than in the early 1970s and
late 1960s.   Although the decline was reversed by heavy external borrowing
in 1976-77, many LDCs are potentially vulnerable to any adverse shift in
their export earnings or to any significant change in their access to
external credit.   More immediately the forty or so most seriously affected
(MSA) countries, those listed by the United Nations as worst affected by
the end-1973 oil price rise, have been unable to borrow very much on international markets.   Their lack of creditworthiness and acute financing needs
have led to a serious resource-transfer problem for the international
community.

However, the seriousness of (non-oil) LDC problems should be kept
in perspective.   As a group they have traditionally been major net
importers of goods and services and net recipients of foreign capital and
aid on a substantial scale.   Since 1973-74 the main change in this pattern
has been a shift in the ultimate source of financing — from industrial
countries to OPEC savings — rather than in the relative size of the

aggregate LDC current deficit.   Following the sizeable increase in t╵
deficit to $29.5 billion in 1974 and $38.2 billion in 1975, it declined
sharply to $25.8 billion in 1976, mainly as a result of domestic adjustment
measures and a modest revival in world trade.   The figure remained at
around this level in 1977 which, after allowing for world economic growth
and inflation, was similar to the 1967-72 annual average.   Some LDCs have
expanded their trade with OPEC as well as with industrial countries in the
past two years while others, such as India and Korea, have benefited from
the repatriation of earnings in OPEC countries.   According to de Vries
(1977) many LDCs have 'beneficially participated' in the adjustment
process in a 'significant way'.

        At the same time there are sharp regional differences.   In Asia
the larger non-oil LDCs adopted effective stabilisation policies in 1974-
75 which have been reinforced by a strong revival in export earnings following the recovery in industrial countries and a rise in world commodity
prices.   As a group these countries are relatively well placed with the
lowest inflation rates and projected strongest growth for any developing
area.   In Latin America and the Caribbean restrictive policies were only
implemented in late 1975-76 after initial attempts had been made to
sustain domestic activity through expansionary fiscal and monetary policies financed by heavy commercial bank borrowing.   The resultant acceler-
ation in inflation rates and growing external deficits were checked in
1977-78 by a combination of domestic restraint, exchange rate depreciation
and higher export prices.   But the scale of external borrowing was not
reduced and debt-service ratios have risen to historically high levels in
a number of countries.

        Economic conditions are least favourable in the non-oil LDCs of
Africa and the Middle East where adjustment has been minimal.   Growth
rates have remained low, inflation is unduly high and the 1977 current
account deficit for these two regions was close to its 1975 peak.   Many
African countries such as Zaire, Zambia and the Sudan face severe debt-
service problems and, in the absence of domestic stabilisation programmes,
there is a danger of more widespread use of trade and payments restrictions.
In the Middle East the major non-oil developing countries have been unable
to implement corrective policies for fear of the political and social
consequences.

        In general, therefore, the international adjustment process is at
a critical stage.   Large external imbalances persist within the various
country groups and are likely to continue in the medium term.   As the
experience of the last few years has shown, delays in dealing with them
could prove costly and there is a clear need for the IMF and other international organisations such as the OECD to guide countries towards more
appropriate policies.

The growth of protection

        The danger of their not doing so is demonstrated by the increasing
resort to protectionist policies which by mid-1978 covered some $100 billion
of trade and affected many industrial countries already hit by a combination
of cyclical and structural problems.   According to the GATT (as reported
in *The Economist* of 24 September 1977), 'the spread of protectionist
pressures may well prove to be the most important current development in
international economic policies for it has reached a point at which the

continued existence of an international order based on agreed and observed rules may be said to be open to question'.

As yet protection has been confined to a few seriously depressed industries but the list has widened in 1977-78 to include steel, textiles and shipbuilding. In the United States a number of orderly market arrangements have been negotiated with low-cost exporters covering colour televisions (Japan), non-rubber shoes (Taiwan and South Korea) and textiles (Hong Kong). Of equal significance was the introduction, in February 1978, of a reference price system for steel imports based on the production costs of the cheapest foreign supplier (Japan). Immediate anti-dumping procedures are initiated if steel import prices fall below the reference price. The aim is to allow home producers to recapture 20% of the domestic steel market.

The EEC has taken similar action on steel in the form of its own reference price system, again based on Japanese production costs. (Even Japan may act against its LDC competitors in 1978-79.) The EEC has also negotiated voluntary restraint agreements with individual suppliers aimed at restricting them to their 1976 share (some 10% overall) of the EEC steel market. Similar agreements have been established with thirty-two countries, including Hong Kong, Taiwan and South Korea, covering over 60% of EEC textile imports. If successful, these agreements will drastically reduce the growth in import volume of certain 'sensitive' products over the next four years.

Finally the depression in the world shipbuilding industry, with the prospect of 30% excess capacity by 1980, has prompted a vicious circle of uneconomic price-cutting and equally uneconomic government subsidies concerned only with short-term employment. (The United Kingdom is a case in point.) The chances of a co-ordinated international strategy are remote and the EEC countries have already rejected Commission plans for a phased reduction in shipbuilding capacity. Japan has agreed to raise export prices and cut capacity but it has not accepted OECD proposals to share new shipbuilding orders on a fifty-fifty basis with other OECD countries. Even in Sweden, one of the few countries to have adopted a medium-term rather than a short-term strategy, there has been substantial building for stock and expensive subsidies including low cost, government-guaranteed loans to encourage orders.

In short, protection or 'managed' free trade is almost respectable again. The various measures have adversely affected growth and debt-servicing prospects in many non-oil LDCs and will contribute to the expected large increase in their aggregate current account deficit in 1978-79. More generally, protection has tied up resources in unproductive uses and inhibited the investment necessary for basic structural adjustments in industrial countries. There is scope here for the IMF in its consultations and in its lending conditions to help check what Long, Secretary-General of the GATT, has called (*The Times*, 23 February 1978) the 'decline in morality' in international trade relations and to work out a co-ordinated approach to one important aspect of the problem, namely the erosion of the industrial countries' traditional markets as a result of the rapid industrialisation of lower cost competitors.

CHAPTER FIVE

FINANCING THE IMBALANCE

The period since 1972 has witnessed the emergence of serious balance of payments problems in many countries, exacerbated in recent months by exchange rate instability and protectionist measures. The unprecedented scale of current account deficits has resulted in a rapid and sizeable accumulation of external debts which in one sense was unavoidable, since adequate short-term adjustment would have involved draconian measures disruptive of world trade and of domestic social and political unity. This chapter looks at the way in which the aggregate deficits have been financed and, in particular, at the major role played by the commercial banks.

General trends

Two general factors stand out. One is the unparalleled size of country borrowing since 1973. Morgan Guaranty (December 1977) estimated that at end-1976 it amounted to $180 billion for non-oil LDCs alone and this figure had risen to well over $200 billion by end-1977. The second is the dramatic change in the form of country borrowing, particularly the growing importance of market borrowing, notably from the commercial banks. An important aspect of this shift for both LDCs and relatively well-developed borrowers has been the shortening of maturity schedules and the higher interest costs (in comparison with more traditional flows) which have brought about disproportionate increases in debt-service payments to be charged against export receipts and new capital inflows.

Non-debt flows (grant aid and equity capital) have not kept pace with rising needs and their relative importance has declined compared with commercial lending. In the six years prior to 1974 grant aid and equity capital accounted for over half of non-oil LDC current account financing but their share in the total dropped abruptly in 1974-76 despite a moderate rise in absolute terms. The industrial countries have consistently failed to meet the UNCTAD aid target of 0.7% of GNP per annum and OPEC aid has been directed almost exclusively to a narrow group of Moslem countries.

Similarly, as Kirbyshire (1977) has shown, the official international institutions have had a very limited intermediary role. Of the $142 billion aggregate OPEC surplus in the three years 1974-76, $50 billion (35%) went into world-wide bank deposits, $25 billion (18%) into bilateral inter-government loans and only $10 billion (7%) into the IMF and IBRD. On the deficit side most of the $50 billion aggregate current deficit of minor OECD countries in this period was financed by bank borrowing as was

$45 billion (58%) of the aggregate non-oil LDC deficit. This was four times the amount financed by IMF and IBRD loans to non-oil LDCs. In 1975-76 the banks provided half of the total credit flows to non-oil LDCs and at end-1976 some two-fifths ($75 billion) of the outstanding external debt of this group was owed to commercial banks.

Bank lending: advantages

Not surprisingly supervisory authorities in several countries, especially the United States, have become increasingly worried about the risks involved in international bank lending, not least the possibility that the large and rising volume of loans to non-oil LDCs could threaten the stability of the international financial system. The risks are considerable, but several mitigating factors should also be taken into account, as set out below.

The recycling role of the commercial banks was a natural one in the context of a net switch from industrial countries to CPEC as the major source of international credit after 1973. The OPEC countries had little alternative but to use the banking systems of industrial countries as a principal outlet for their surpluses: and since balance of payments financing needs have far outstripped the amounts available from official sources the intermediation of the commercial banks has helped to sustain world trade and economic activity.

International lending standards have been generally high following the collapse of Franklin National and Herstatt in 1974. Contrary to popular belief, loan loss experience in international lending has been considerably better than in domestic lending for the US banks (which account for the bulk of country loans and for which up-to-date data are available). According to Costanzo (1975), 'not one cent' has been written off for balance of payments reasons since 1945. From 1971 to 1975 — according to a special *IMF Survey* report on international lending (June 1977) — the international loan loss ratio for the largest US banks was only one-third of the loan loss ratio on total loans and, although losses rose on all categories of loans in 1975-76, those on international loans rose substantially less than on domestic loans. Rescheduling is fairly common for US banks, particularly among Latin American borrowers, but there were only two cases per year in the three years 1975 to 1977, compared with six in 1972. Several major banks will not now lend or restructure loans without some guarantee of improved economic performance, increasingly in the form of an IMF standby.

It is also easy to overstate the degree of risk in banks' international operations. A substantial proportion of international claims, especially to the higher-risk LDCs, are self-liquidating trade credits. In addition a large number of bank claims on non-oil LDCs are guaranteed by official entities and private corporations in the country of the lending bank or another industrial country. The risk in these transactions is borne not by the banks but elsewhere.

International lending by the commercial banks has contributed significantly to their earnings at a time when loan demand in the industrial countries has been depressed by recession. For example, the international earnings of the thirteen largest US banks increased at an annual rate of 36% between 1970 and 1975 and accounted for nearly half of these banks'

total earnings in 1975.   More recently the greater part of the rise in
1977 earnings at Manufacturers Hanover Trust and Morgan Guaranty, two of
the largest US banks, has been attributed to overseas lending.   In
general the rate of profitability has also been higher for US banks in
foreign rather than domestic ventures.

Lastly, but perhaps most importantly, the US banks have been very
selective about the countries to whom they lend and loans to LDCs form
only a small proportion of the total.   This can be seen from Table 5.1
which covers total foreign lending by all US banks at end-1976.

At end-1976 the largest share of US bank foreign assets represented claims on the Group of Ten countries and Switzerland and on offshore
banking centres which together amounted to $125 billion (60%).   The over-
whelming proportion of the $45 billion in claims on non-oil LDCs was con-
centrated in the higher income, higher growth members of this group with
the most favourable long-term prospects.   Loans to Mexico and Brazil each
accounted for about a quarter of this sub-total and the rest was mainly to
countries with long-standing economic links with the United States, Korea,
Taiwan, the Philippines and Latin American borrowers.   Loans to the
highly publicised 'problem' LDCs were relatively small — for example,
only $0.2 billion was outstanding to Zaire.

The same selectivity is apparent in two more recent surveys.   In
August 1977 the *Federal Reserve Bank of New York Quarterly Review* reported
that, of the $180 billion lent to non-oil LDCs at end-1976 by official and
private lenders, 30% went to Brazil and Mexico, 12% to Argentina, Chile,
Colombia and Peru and a further 12% to Korea, the Philippines, Taiwan and
Thailand.   As before, banks' exposure to country risks was limited and
normally concentrated in 'healthy' LDCs.   Similarly a comprehensive study
of the foreign operations of the 119 largest US banks by the US regulatory
agencies found that 40% of the $164 billion lent by these banks at end-June
1977 went to the Group of Ten and Switzerland.   Mexico and Brazil took
over half of the $40 billion outstanding to non-oil LDCs, the 'problem'
African countries less than $2 billion.

In sum, fears of widespread default are probably unjustified,
especially given the improvement in the balance of payments position of
many LDCs since 1975 and the competent handling of the problem cases such
as North Korea and Zaire.

Bank lending: disadvantages

However, there have been several problems which seem likely to
become more acute unless there is a better mix of official and private
financing which looks ahead to medium-term requirements.   The banks need
the support of official (IMF) arrangements with economic conditions
attached which will allow countries in difficulties to progress to more
sustainable balance of payments positions.

The appropriateness of bank lending has been increasingly ques-
tioned in areas where it does not appear suited to the nature of different
financing needs.   For example, bank loans after 1974 have been used to
fund structural development projects with a pay-back period well in excess
of the five to seven year euromarket norm.   In consequence some countries
face growing refinancing requirements which will add considerably to their

Table 5.1   Claims on foreign countries of head offices and foreign branches of US banks, December 1976

$ billion

G.10 and Switzerland		
Belgium-Luxembourg	6.1	
France	10.0	
Germany	8.8	
Italy	5.8	
Netherlands	2.8	
Sweden	1.3	
Switzerland	3.0	
United Kingdom	41.4	
Canada	5.1	
Japan	15.8	100.1
Other developed countries		15.1
OPEC countries		
Ecuador	0.7	
Venezuela	4.1	
Indonesia	2.2	
Middle East countries	4.2	
African countries	1.5	12.7
Non-oil developing countries		
Brazil	11.8	
Mexico	11.5	
Korea	3.1	
Philippines	2.2	
Taiwan	2.4	
Other	14.2	45.2
Eastern Europe		5.2
Offshore banking centres		23.9
Miscellaneous and unallocated		5.1
Total		207.3

Source: Attachment to Statement of Governor Henry C. Wallich (before the Subcommittee on Financial Institutions, Supervision, Regulation and Insurance of the Committee on Banking, Finance and Urban Affairs of the US House of Representatives, Washington DC, 23 March 1977)

Note: Data are adjusted to exclude claims of US agencies and branches of foreign banks on listed countries and to exclude accounts between offices of the same parent bank. No adjustment can be made to exclude claims of one US bank or its overseas branches on an overseas branch of another US bank.

gross credit demands.   Refinancing could also become increasingly important because of the concentration of maturing debt, incurred immediately
after the 1973 oil price rise, in 1978-80.   According to the *Amex Bank
Review* (March 1977), over half of gross eurocurrency borrowing by non-oil
LDCs in 1980 will be to refinance existing debts.   By 1985 some two-
thirds of such borrowing will be for eurodebt repayments — hardly an
encouraging prospect for banks.

       Refinancing could have adverse implications for international
banks with regard to the matching of assets and liabilities by maturity
and by currency.   The banks could be forced — as the only alternative to
default — to roll over balance of payments loans for periods of 10, 15 or
even 20 years, which might involve unforeseeable political and exchange
rate risks.   It would also tie up large sums and limit the banks' ability
to lend in more attractive markets.   This in turn might increase banks'
reluctance to lend further to certain countries, however viable the particular project, a trend which could be reinforced by the tightening up of
controls on such lending by the supervisory authorities.

       On a related issue the structure of the international banks'
balance sheets has changed radically since 1973.   The major banks were
previously able to spread their risks by dealing with a large number of
borrowers and depositors and by acting as both debtor and creditor in the
case of large corporate or country customers.   The pattern has now shifted
with OPEC deposits concentrated in relatively few banks and recycled in
large loans to a small group of country borrowers.   This has subjected
some banks' capital adequacy ratios to considerable strain and left them
increasingly vulnerable to a single large default.

       Despite selective lending policies, the cumulative effects of
the oil imbalance have left some banks at or very near the limits of
prudent credit risk in relation to individual oil importers.   In Peru,
for example, the economy has been badly hit by the decline in world copper
prices and the exhaustion of anchovy meal exports.   In 1977 the current
account deficit was $0.85 billion, only just below the record $1.0 billion
in 1976, and foreign exchange reserves were actually negative.   By early
1978 *Euromoney* (March 1978) reported that Peru's outstanding medium-term
debt totalled just over $4 billion: debt-service payments (principal and
interest) amounted to $0.9 billion in 1978, 45% of forecast export earnings,
and were expected to rise to over $1 billion in 1979 and 1980.   Access to
commercial bank credit in 1977-78 was jeopardised by the authorities'
refusal to take the necessary adjustment measures.   In November 1977 an
SDR 90 million standby was ratified by the IMF but the second instalment was
not released in March 1978 as scheduled because of questionable accounting
procedures and failure to keep to agreed budgetary targets.   Peru's options
are now strictly limited, since further bank lending is dependent on the
government's ability to satisfy the IMF.

       There may also be repayment problems in some eastern European
countries.   A BIS survey, reported in *Financial Times* of 15 June 1977,
found that commercial bank debts totalled over $25 billion, half of which
were due for repayment in 1977.   Total liabilities considerably exceeded
unused credit facilities and deposits with western banks.   Although the
debts were not large in international perspective and COMECON has a good
repayment record, Poland was one country which found it difficult to
secure new loans in 1977-78 because of a persistent trade deficit and a
relatively high level of outstanding debt.   More generally, little

improvement is expected in eastern Europe's chronic trade deficit with the west in the medium term. USSR grain imports are forecast to rise sharply and planned export targets may not be reached as a result of the slow recovery in world trade and the widespread introduction of protectionist measures.

In Africa, the Sudan is an example of a country to which the international banks lent fairly heavily in 1973-74 without adequate analysis of over-ambitious development projects or future export earnings. *Euromoney* (March 1978) reported that in early 1978 external debt totalled $1.8 billion, excluding OPEC loans, of which $0.4 billion was owed to commercial banks. The government was already up to a year behind on most of its repayment schedules and, although the banks were keen to avoid outright default, the chances of prompt repayment, with official reserves then equivalent to only 1% of outstanding debt, were virtually non-existent. As in the case of Peru, the government's medium-term prospects depend on an IMF approved stabilisation programme which could encourage rescheduling by the banks and other creditors.

In other parts of the world, bank lending to minor OECD countries such as Turkey and Portugal seems very large when set against immediate economic prospects. Indeed the main financing problems in the period to 1982 could involve countries in this group. In Turkey, particularly, the possibility of substantial default was (in mid-1978) a real one unless the government could effectively implement IMF recommendations to cut inflation (running at 40-50% at an annual rate in 1977) and reduce the record $2.84 billion current deficit. In early 1978 total external debt amounted to $15 billion (50% of 1977 GNP) of which some $5-6 billion was to commercial banks. In 1977 the government defaulted on $0.4 billion of commercial bank loans and a further $1 billion of these were scheduled to mature in 1978. According to *Euromoney* (March 1978) some $4 billion or so was required in new foreign loans merely to service overdue and maturing debts in 1978 — and the US Export-Import Bank had already extended the repayment period on loans worth $25 million. Successful debt rescheduling in the medium term depends on the restoration of international confidence in the Turkish economy through the IMF. At least a start has been made with the austerity measures of early 1978 which included a substantial devaluation of the lira.

A principal attraction of bank finance has been its relative anonymity and its virtual lack of conditions. In theory market discipline, in the form of bank loans paid out in instalments which are subject to a review of the borrower's economic performance, can have some effect in ensuring that loans are used effectively. In practice most banks have neither the inclination nor the leverage to impose restrictions on sovereign governments. They are not equipped for direct policy involvement which could involve conflict not only with the borrowing government but with other creditors, including official creditors, whose economic prescriptions might be different. Banks also risk being drawn into a continuing responsibility for the success of policies agreed.

This situation is in no-one's longer term interest. Variation in bank interest rates has contributed only marginally to adjustment — indeed the attraction of higher interest rates in Zaire pushed banks to imprudent limits in 1973-75. There were signs also in the mid-1977-mid-1978 period of a re-emergence of a borrower's market in country loans because many banks were very liquid due to the weakness of private loan demand in industrial countries. Increasing competition among banks, notably from Japanese and European lenders, led to tighter lending margins (well below 1%), longer maturities (many over seven years) and pressures on banks to relax the provisions concerning legal safeguards on new loans. Less than prime borrowers (non-oil LDCs) obtained considerably better terms in early 1978 than was possible a year before and there were several instances, including Malaysia and the Philippines, of outstanding loans being renegotiated to take advantage of lower margins.

The easing of terms may lead to future problems for the banks, particularly in view of the large amounts involved. (A record $36 billion was borrowed in medium-term eurocredits in 1977 alone.) There is no likelihood either that the demand will diminish given the projected pattern of payments deficits, large-scale refinancing needs and the continuation of development and investment programmes such as that associated with North Sea oil. The only way of avoiding a future Turkey or Peru is through greater IMF involvement, since the Fund has the authority to impose conditions on its lending which, if effectively followed, can provide a reasonable guarantee that bank loans will be repaid. (This possibility is developed more fully in Chapters Six and Eight.)

A further drawback is that the international banks have been lending to countries on the basis of incomplete, inaccurate and out of date information. Country data on total indebtedness, maturity profile and the interest burden are often not collected. National sources vary widely in coverage and promptness from the regular, comprehensive breakdowns of major industrial countries, to COMECON which publishes no figures at all. The main sources for information on LDC debt are international institutions: the IBRD, which collects data on public and public-guaranteed debt in 86 developing countries; the IMF, which publishes regular information on the use of its resources; and the BIS, which produces quarterly figures showing external claims, on individual LDCs, by banks in G.10 countries and Switzerland and offshore branches of US banks. There are numerous gaps in coverage. The IBRD figures do not cover short-term external liabilities or obligations to non-residents incurred in the currency of the debtor country, although they are rapidly being expanded to cover non-guaranteed private flows. The BIS does not give a complete country breakdown and excludes banks (and branches) in countries outside its reporting system. There are also problems of comparability since countries use different categories to allocate the various forms of debt — public and private, short and long-term.

This has inevitably made it difficult for banks to assess the risks attached to international loans. All the major banks have developed their own sophisticated credit-rating systems and at Bank of America, for example, quantitative analysis of economic data is supplemented by comprehensive review of political, social and historical factors to establish short and long-term ratings and set maximum exposure limits. However, exposure is not always easy to measure since definitions vary among banks, as does the form of bank lending which ranges from short-term export credit to long-term development loans. Similarly, evaluation depends mainly on subjective interpretation of incomplete data and there are no 'correct' levels of reserves or of the debt-service ratio to guide banks.

The attitude of supervisory authorities

Official policy in several lending countries, notably the United States, has moved towards greater control of banks' international operations since 1976. US banks have been encouraged to keep the growth in

international loans commensurate with the expansion of individual borrowers' debt-servicing capabilities and the accent has been on safety and
higher lending standards. Federal Reserve Board supervision has been
extended to cover exchange rate and country risks; and more frequent (and
more detailed) collection of foreign loan data has also been introduced.

More specifically Heimman, the Comptroller of Currency, acted in
1978 to tighten the regulations covering loans to foreign governments and
their agencies. Since January 1978 — as reported in *Financial Times* of
9 January — these loans have been treated together under the law which
provides that a bank may not lend more than 10% of its capital to a single
borrower, unless a 'means' test and a 'purpose' test can be met. The
means test stipulates that the borrower must have sufficient resources or
income of its own, over time, to service its debt obligations; the
purpose test that loan proceeds must be used by the borrower in the con-
duct of its business and for the purpose represented in the loan agreement
or otherwise acknowledged in writing by the borrower. Banks are required
to keep full documentary evidence (including financial statements and
credit assessments) justifying individual lending decisions in these cases.
If the tests cannot be met, loans by a bank to 'foreign governments, their
agencies and instrumentalities' will not be allowed, in aggregate, to
exceed the 10% ceiling. In outstanding cases these loans might have to
be reduced over an agreed period to bring them under 10%. There have been
indications in the press that informal loan requests from eastern European
countries, which normally borrow overseas through one public agency, were
refused in 1978 under this ruling.

At the same time the US regulatory agencies (Federal Reserve Board,
Federal Deposit Insurance Corporation, and Comptroller's Office) have
agreed on the outlines of a new co-ordinated system for monitoring banks'
foreign lending. The most important elements include a common reporting
form and revised procedures for measuring banks' foreign loan exposure,
with emphasis on identifying any concentration in lending which seems large
in relation to bank capital or to conditions in the recipient country. The
details of the system were under discussion in mid-1978.

On the other hand, the US regulatory agencies are also aware of the
need for the international banks to continue lending, since a sudden con-
traction, whether because of a revival in industrial countries' loan demand
or an over-reaction to creditworthiness considerations, might have damaging
consequences. Significantly the new proposals for supervising banks'
foreign lending rule out uniform criteria for loan evaluation by banks or
the possibility of assigning credit ratings to individual countries. As
Wallich (1977), Federal Reserve Board, has argued, excessive restriction
of banks might impede the 'necessary rollovers and desirable new inflows'
thereby provoking the defaults that bank supervision is supposed to guard
against. It might also discourage banks marginally involved in foreign
lending from continuing and place an additional burden on the larger banks.

In conclusion it seems likely that the major banks will continue
to be actively involved in foreign lending, albeit at a slower pace, for
the foreseeable future. According to Nash (1977), vice-president of
Morgan Guaranty, net bank exposure in non-oil LDCs is projected to increase
at an annual rate of 10% in the period 1978-80, compared with an average
annual rate of 40% since 1974. The potential problems would be considerably eased by an extension of conditional IMF credit and renewed emphasis
on medium-term adjustment in borrowing countries.

CHAPTER SIX

THE ROLE OF THE IMF: ADJUSTMENT

The need for a stronger IMF seems indisputable and this chapter examines the ways in which the IMF can extend its influence over members' adjustment policies with regard to consultations, persuasion, exchange rate supervision and lending conditions. Of these the last two have the most far-reaching implications.

It is, however, worth mentioning at the outset that the IMF is not the only forum for co-ordinating international adjustment. Its work is supplemented by other international organisations such as the General Agreement on Tariffs and Trade (GATT), the Organisation for Economic Co-operation and Development (OECD) and the European Economic Community (EEC), whose functions are outlined below.

Other international institutions and adjustment

The GATT is a multilateral treaty established in 1947 which is designed to have a similar role to the IMF, but in the sphere of inter-national trade. There are a number of legal links between the GATT and the IMF and the two organisations co-operate closely in pursuit of a co-ordinated international approach to trade and payments restrictions. Informal consultations and exchanges of information are fairly common and the one is usually represented at the other's important meetings.

The aims of the GATT are to ensure that international trade is conducted in a non-discriminatory manner and that protection of domestic industries, when necessary, is effected through customs tariffs rather than import quotas or other direct controls. The Contracting Parties to the GATT are only permitted to introduce quantitative restrictions in very exceptional circumstances. The principle of non-discrimination means that such restrictions must be applied to all trading partners, not just against one particular country.

Mainly because of the inflexibility of these 'safeguard' clauses the GATT Articles have been increasingly ignored since the early 1970s. The use of export subsidies and other non-tariff barriers to trade has become widespread, notably among industrial countries, but so far the Contracting Parties have failed to agree on more realistic GATT procedures for consultation, dispute settlement and temporary safeguards subject to international surveillance. At the same time the GATT discussions to reduce tariffs, the so-called Tokyo Round, have had only limited success. After five years of negotiation agricultural tariffs remain a controversial area and the consensus reached in mid-1978 to cut tariffs on industrial

goods by 35-40% in the 1980-88 period falls well short of original hopes.
Even here the United States, the EEC and Japan have claimed exemptions in
important areas and some EEC members have advocated an escape clause in
the final agreement which would allow governments to postpone those
tariff reductions due after 1985 if economic conditions are 'unfavourable'.

In short the GATT framework has proved largely ineffective in
preventing the drift towards protection.   The impact of the Tokyo Round
concessions will be spread over the next decade and the use of non-tariff
restrictions has become an accepted part of national economic strategies.
This in turn has placed a greater burden on the IMF to direct adjustment
into more appropriate channels.

The OECD was established in 1960 by the 24 leading industrial and
advanced primary-producing countries.   Its principal aim is to promote
economic growth in member countries and thereby contribute to the expansion
of world trade and world economic development.   The main decision-making
organ is the Council of Ministers, composed of members' economics and
finance ministers, which meets periodically under the chairmanship of an
appointed Secretary-General.   The Council is advised by specialist committees of national experts and much of the necessary research and economic
analysis is done by a permanent international secretariat, based in Paris,
whose role is broadly similar to that of the IMF staff.

The influence of the OECD in international adjustment originated
in the growing inflexibility of the Bretton Woods system in the early
1960s, particularly the lack of clear guidelines over which countries
should initiate adjustment.   The OECD, rather than the IMF, was the
natural forum for consultations because the problems were of primary
concern to the major (OECD) countries and could be discussed at a more
senior level than in the IMF Executive Board.   In 1961 an Economic Policy
Committee (EPC) of finance ministers was established to monitor developments in members' economies, with particular reference to 'the international
effects of national policies', and the Committee in turn set up four working
parties of finance ministry and central bank officials.   The most influential is Working Party Number 3 (WP3) which meets every six weeks and has
representatives from Canada, France, West Germany, Italy, Japan, Netherlands,
Sweden, Switzerland, the United Kingdom and the United States.   Its
official function as set out in the list of OECD bodies (1977) is 'to analyse the effects on international payments of monetary, fiscal and other
policy measures and to consult together on policy measures, both national
and international, as they relate to international payments equilibrium'.

The effectiveness of the EPC framework is hard to measure.   According to Williamson (1977) the WP3 meetings have widely been judged valuable in developing understanding and even at times making a modest contribution to consistency.   Since 1976-77 WP3 has been a key forum for the,
as yet unsuccessful, attempt by the major countries to agree on a concerted strategy for world economic growth.   There has certainly been no
shortage of ideas.   In March 1978, for example, WP3 examined proposals
that recovery in the United States should be supported by reflation in the
'locomotive' countries of West Germany and Japan and also, to a more limited
extent, in a group of 'convalescent' countries — France, Italy, the United
Kingdom and Sweden.   On the other hand, as in the IMF and elsewhere,
national interests and national policy freedom have rarely, if ever, been
subordinated to the benefit of other countries with different priorities
and objectives.   WP3 has no sanctions except moral suasion; and major
differences of opinion can only be papered over.

The main contribution of the OECD Secretariat is one of independent forecasting and policy prescription. The Secretariat produces regular surveys of members' economies, similar in form to the annual reports of the IMF staff, and also publishes a six-monthly *Economic Outlook* which analyses members' targets and contains recommendations for mutually consistent stable growth. In December 1977, for example, the Secretariat stressed the need for 'differentiation' in members' 1978 policies, with the emphasis on greater fiscal stimulus in surplus countries. In the longer term the July 1976 *Outlook* included a 'growth scenario to 1980', endorsed by OECD Ministers, with the aim of providing 'a quantitative framework' for future policies. But members have already fallen well short of the growth, inflation and unemployment targets; and the scenario is now of doubtful relevance.

More concrete initiatives by the OECD Secretariat have come to very little, one example being the virtually defunct Financial Support Fund which is examined more fully in Chapter Seven. The 1974 trade pledge, an undertaking by members to avoid unilateral trade and current account restrictions, has had some effect in encouraging consultations on trade policies within the OECD, but it has proved an ineffective barrier to protectionist pressures in 1976-78. Its value has been undermined by the widespread use of subsidies and other non-tariff barriers among OECD members, many of which face severe structural problems because of LDC competition in basic industries as explained in Chapter Four. As in the adjustment sphere generally, the Secretariat is hampered by the absence of control procedures and the fact that the problems can no longer be comprehensively dealt with in a forum which excludes OPEC and other important primary producers.

The EEC provides another forum in which the leading European countries can discuss common economic problems and work towards closer policy co-ordination. The influence of the EEC Commission, the central organisation of the Community, is backed by a number of short- to medium-term support facilities (described more fully in Chapter Seven) and several longer-term financing mechanisms, such as the European Investment Bank and the Regional Development Fund. In addition, four of the nine member countries participate in a joint currency float against the US dollar and other major currencies ('the snake') which is managed under the auspices of the European Monetary Co-operation Fund. The ultimate aim of the Community, as set out in the 1972 Werner Report, remains that of complete economic and monetary union, although this seems an increasingly long-term goal in view of the persistent wide divergences in members' balance of payments positions, growth and inflation rates.

In recent years the Commission has established a network of specialist committees to deal with the whole range of adjustment policies including monetary and fiscal developments, European trade and energy conservation. One of the most influential is the Monetary Committee, composed of senior finance ministry and central bank officials, which meets regularly to review short-term objectives and monitor declared targets. In April 1978 the Committee's chairman, Van Ypersele, played an important part in initiating proposals for a more interventionist EEC exchange rate system, as outlined below. At the same time an Economic Policy Committee has attempted to establish consistent growth policies within an agreed overall strategy. As one example, the Copenhagen meeting of heads of governments in April 1978 endorsed a target of 4-4½% average growth in the year to mid-1979.

The EEC's influence, however, like that of the OECD and the GATT, has been limited by the lack of political will on the part of its members and by the absence of effective sanctions on errant countries. While the IMF shares some of the weaknesses of these three organisations, it is in a stronger position to affect countries' adjustment policies because of its wider membership, broader powers of surveillance and financial authority.

The IMF and adjustment

(a) Consultations

In general terms the IMF reform exercise at least reaffirmed the principle of international co-operation, through the Fund, in monetary affairs. According to Witteveen (1976), speaking as IMF Managing Director, the 1978 Amendments to the IMF Articles demonstrate that 'the collapse of the Bretton Woods system did not mean that nations wished to abandon the idea of a monetary system based on international obligations internationally administered'. The Amendments should help the IMF, legally, to extend its co-ordinating role through the well-established system of regular consultations with members, which form an integral part of the Fund's work and the instrument for surveillance of agreed policies. They provide a valuable external appraisal of members' economies and allow members to raise difficulties arising from other countries' actions. They also enable the IMF to keep up to date with developments in individual countries and deal promptly with requests for financial assistance. The information acquired is used as the basis for general policy decisions and as background for much of the other work of the Fund — for example the Annual Report on Exchange Restrictions.

All Article XIV countries are obliged to consult annually with the IMF and consultations are held on a voluntary basis with the 43 Article VIII countries. Consultations are supplemented by quarterly 'mini-consultations' with the major industrial members, which permit closer monitoring of the multilateral aspects of their policies. In addition, frequent consultations are normally required when a member has borrowed from the IMF. The importance of consultations is shown by the fact that the Executive Board spent some fifty per cent more time discussing country matters in 1975-76 than in 1969-70.

(b) Sanctions

On the other hand the Amended Articles do not include additional incentives or pressures to back up advice given by the Fund in its discussions with individual countries. As before there are a number of general obligations imposed on members, but the IMF still lacks the power to impose material sanctions except on countries that need its financial assistance. In the case of surplus countries or reserve centres in deficit the Fund has very limited weight, not least because of the failure to strengthen the already anachronistic scarce currency clauses (outlined in Chapter Two) in the Amended Article VII. The difficulties of invoking this Article, both political and technical, remain considerable and since it has never been used there are no established criteria by which the Fund can deem a currency scarce. In the case of a scarcity of IMF holdings of a particular currency the IMF will have various alternatives, such as borrowing from the member or requiring the member to sell its currency to the Fund for SDRs (Amended Article VII, 1), before instituting exchange restrictions and other sanctions.

There would be similar difficulties if the IMF were to consider publishing reports on members' 'monetary or economic conditions' or on 'developments which directly tend to produce a serious disequilibrium in the international balance of payments of members' (Amended Article XII, 8). In theory such action could exert pressure to comply with Fund advice by promoting currency speculation or discriminatory trade controls. However, it is precisely these methods which make this sanction difficult to employ and its activation requires a 70% majority in the Executive Board. The extreme penalty of declaring a member ineligible to use IMF resources (Amended Article V, 5) would be an ineffective deterrent for surplus countries. On past evidence it is unlikely to be invoked except as a last resort if a member is seriously misusing Fund credit.

(c) Persuasion

Surplus countries and errant reserve centres therefore remain in a far better position to avoid their adjustment responsibilities than deficit countries which are now more than ever dependent on the amount and terms of available finance. To a large extent adjustment by surplus countries will depend on nudging by their peers and the IMF and on their own recognition of the possible contractionary effects on the world economy if deficit countries are left with an excessive adjustment burden.

IMF nudging has taken several constructive forms, not least in the matter of forging stronger links with the OPEC group, which could aid the transition towards a more stable international order. The influence of this group will be critical in three main areas — oil pricing, investment of oil revenues and aid. If, for example, the oil producers attempted to compensate for their declining surpluses by large price increases, the adjustment efforts of oil importers and the IMF could be nullified. However, since 1973-74 OPEC has followed a reasonably responsible pricing policy; and the excess world supply of oil in 1978 has led to a price freeze at least until early 1979.

Despite early fears, OPEC investments have not disrupted western financial markets and considerable diversification has taken place since 1974. Short-term investment has taken more varied forms and been placed with a wider group of financial institutions. OPEC funds have also gone increasingly into equities, corporate bonds and real estate. According to Witteveen (1977), total medium- and long-term OPEC investments in 1974 accounted for 32% of the cash surplus, but the proportion rose to 65% in 1975 and 73% in 1976. Between mid-1977 and mid-1978 there was evidence — hardly surprising in view of the dollar's depreciation — of a switch of OPEC assets into other currencies. The *Bank of England Quarterly Bulletin* (March 1978) estimated that total OPEC investment in the United States in 1977, at $8.9 billion, was some 25% lower than in 1976.

On a fairly modest scale the IMF has helped to direct the OPEC surplus into relatively stable channels through the provision of appropriate recycling mechanisms. Examples include the 1974-75 oil facilities and the proposed supplementary financing facility which are examined in Chapter Seven. In addition the OPEC share in Fund quotas has also been increased and the oil producers are starting to play an increasingly active role in IMF management.   There is scope for the IMF, in its consultations, to support a more direct transfer of finance from OPEC to borrowing countries through equity and bond markets or through inter-government lending.   A shift in project financing from a fixed debt to an equity basis could alleviate the debt problems of several LDCs.   There is room also for larger and more widely spread aid flows.   Prospects here are mixed, but the doubling of the OPEC Special Aid Fund in 1977 was a hopeful sign.   Although primarily a matter for the World Bank, IMF technical assistance programmes could help to improve the employment of OPEC flows in deficit LDCs.

As already shown in Chapter One the influence of the IMF and of other international organisations on the United States is limited by that country's special position in the world economy.   However, the weakness of the dollar between mid-1977 and mid-1978 caused serious instability in the foreign exchange markets, which in turn had a disruptive effect on the slow recovery of world trade and investment after the 1974-75 recession. Since April 1977 the United States has been subject to the same guidance on exchange rate policy as the other IMF members, and the US-West German support operations in January and March 1978 were in line with the IMF's Exchange Rate Principles set out below.   The US authorities have also indicated their readiness to use their reserve position in the IMF — some $5 billion — in their short-term smoothing operations.

In the longer term the IMF has a responsibility to support, in public, US efforts to remedy its oil deficit since international approval can be a useful weapon for governments when dealing with parliaments and public opinion.   The dilatory approach of the US Congress has aggravated the pressure on oil prices and contributed to the continued high level of the aggregate OPEC surplus.   An effective energy policy in the United States would benefit not only the dollar but international adjustment in general.

The depreciation of the dollar over the year to mid-1978 also reflected sizeable capital outflows from the United States, as explained more fully in Chapter Four.   Despite their economic strength, however, neither West Germany, Japan nor Switzerland showed any wish that their currencies should take over the dollar's reserve currency role, not least because of the possible constraints on domestic policy.   In all three countries stringent exchange controls were used between December 1977 and February 1978 to deter capital inflows.

The international repercussions of the dollar's decline underline the need for an international solution to the problem.   This has not been lessened by the April 1978 US Treasury decision to hold at least six monthly gold auctions, each of 300,000 ounces.   The sales are on too small a scale to have a significant impact on the US trade deficit and thereby strengthen the dollar.   One alternative, discussed inconclusively by the C20 and revived by the IMF Managing Director in 1978, would be the establishment of an IMF Substitution Account through which SDRs might be exchanged for dollars.   Under this sort of scheme SDRs would be allocated to IMF members in proportion to quotas, but at the same time all members, or a large proportion of members, would deposit an equivalent amount of dollars in a special account to be operated by the IMF.   (This could be set up under Amended Article V, 2 which allows the IMF to perform 'financial services' for members.)   The dollars in this account would be invested in US official long-term securities and depositors would receive interest accordingly, but would probably have no right of redemption of their claim, which would be entirely illiquid.

The details of this proposal, not least the number of participants in the substitution operation, the amount of the substitution and the terms to be applied to the substituted dollar balances, would inevitably be controversial. In the first instance, there are strong arguments for excluding LDCs. Their share of an SDR allocation, and therefore of the substitution operation, would be small — less than 25% of the total — and some hard pressed LDCs might, in the short term, dispose of their SDRs for dollars to make trade payments. Exclusion of the LDCs would provide a convenient mechanism for effecting a small redistribution of world reserves. In contrast the major industrial countries and OPEC would receive the bulk, nearly 70%, of a quota-based allocation and would be more likely to retain these SDRs.

The amount of substitution necessary to stabilise the dollar and, in the longer term, promote the SDR would also form a major part of any discussions. It seems unlikely, however, that the agreed amount of dollars to be substituted would initially exceed SDR 5 billion and even this might prove too ambitious for some European countries. Broadly speaking they regard the scheme as offering the United States funding of its debts, without a corresponding increase in US obligations or real advantages for major dollar-holders. For the proposal to be viable the United States might have to offer amortisation of the dollars held in the IMF special account or, at worst, an undated commitment for the future. This seems unlikely given the lukewarm attitude of the US authorities to the whole idea, which may well prevent its effective implementation in the near term.

Even assuming that the position of the dollar improves as a result of the kind of measures outlined above, the United States cannot be expected to maintain the world economic recovery without assistance from well placed countries such as West Germany and Japan. The IMF, in consultations and in the Executive Board, has taken the lead in urging non-inflationary adjustment on these two countries in the form of increased aid flows, broader market access for LDCs and currency revaluation, as described more fully below. Equally important, Witteveen has encouraged longer term policies for surplus countries such as the revival of productive investment to sustain recovery and create the capacity needed in key sectors to meet growing demand.

Nevertheless, IMF influence has been limited by three main factors. The first is the absence of an agreed set of adjustment rules; the second is the feeling, left over from the 1960s, that external surplus is somehow virtuous and deficit sinful; and the third is the historical fear of inflation, particularly in West Germany. So far strong international pressure in the IMF and in other international organisations such as the OECD and EEC has failed to produce any lasting change in the hesitant and cautious reflationary policies of West Germany and Japan. The best that has been achieved by the IMF is a rather vague 'consensus', reached at the April 1978 meeting of the Interim Committee, on the general outlines of a co-ordinated growth strategy for 1979-80 as set out in Table 6.1.

Ideally growth rates in industrial countries would be geared to the amount of slack in the respective domestic economies, the strength of countries' external positions and progress in reducing inflation. The suggested IMF targets imply further stimulation of demand in most industrial countries other than the United States, but the chances of West Germany and Japan complying with these recommendations appeared slight in mid-1978.

Table 6.1   Growth scenario to 1980 - annual or
               annual average increases in real GNP

Percentages

	1963-73	1977	1978 (estimate)	1979-80 (recommended)
United States	4.0	4.9	4.5	4
Japan	10.3	5.1	5.7	7½
West Germany	4.8	2.5	3.1	4½
France	5.9	2.7	3.1	4½
United Kingdom	2.6	0.8	2.9	3½
Canada	5.7	2.6	4.5	5½
Italy	4.8	1.7	2.6	4
Other industrialised countries[1]	4.6	1.9	2.2	4½
Total, industrialised countries	4.8	3.7	4.0	4¾

Source: *Economist Financial Report*, Vol.2, No.49, 18 May 1978

[1]Austria, Belgium, Denmark, Holland, Norway, Sweden and Switzerland

(d) Exchange rates

Since mid-1973 the par value provisions of the IMF Articles have been universally ignored and the 1974 Guidelines for Floating have had little or no effect on members' policies. The Amended Article IV allows more extensive Fund surveillance of exchange rate policies and gives the Fund more scope to ensure that rate changes contribute to international adjustment.

The exchange rate practices of IMF members have varied considerably over the five years to 1978 ranging from independent floating, with little attempt to influence market forces, to the maintenance of a fixed peg against a single intervention currency. Two factors stand out: one that three-quarters of IMF members have continued to maintain a fixed exchange rate relationship of some sort; and the other that floating as practised by the major industrial countries has been subject to a considerable degree of official management.

Among the countries which formally fix their exchange rates, a number of different techniques are used, reflecting historical and institutional as well as economic factors. The most commonly used technique is that of pegging to one currency. In mid-1977, according to the 1977 IMF *Annual Report*, 44 countries had pegged their currencies to the dollar, 14 to the French franc and 9 to other currencies: the exchange rates of a further 7 countries were fixed by the authorities but adjusted frequently on the basis of cost and price indicators. An increasing number of countries, 29 in mid-1977, had linked their currencies to a basket of currencies or the SDR. In addition, five countries (as at April 1978) participated in the European common margins arrangement, the 'snake', under which their currencies were maintained within a narrow band of fluctuation against each other, although not against the currencies of other countries.

Exchange rate policies in the latter countries have also been varied more frequently than before 1973 in the form of new intervention points, repegging and the use of formulae or indicators as a guide to peg changes. In the three years 1974-76, 19 of the 73 'unitary peggers' made one or more changes in their intervention points, which is in sharp contrast to the 1968-70 period when only one country, Canada, changed from a fixed peg to a floating arrangement and only six changes in par value were effected.

Within the group of countries that permit continuous exchange rate flexibility, free floating has never been tried for long. The massive run on the dollar in mid-1973 confirmed the understandable reluctance of governments to lose control over such an important policy variable and was convincing evidence that spot exchange rates demonstrably needed management. Since then the need for intervention has been assumed by most governments, whose main concern has been the appropriate form of influencing exchange rates — official borrowing, exchange controls or monetary policy changes. The extent of intervention has varied widely from short-term smoothing operations (Canada and the minor 'snake' countries) to constant support in countries with difficult payments problems such as the United Kingdom at end-1976.

In general, therefore, it is apparent that a growing diversity of exchange rate policies has been accompanied by a willingness to change exchange arrangements to meet new circumstances. Countries prepared to subordinate domestic policy to the maintenance of a rigidly fixed rate for any appreciable period of time now represent only a small proportion of world trade. The new attitude can be traced to several causes, not least the unstable economic conditions and high level of world inflation since 1972-73. Uncertainty about the structural changes in world trade has led to greater awareness of the exchange rate as an adjustment tool in both an international and a domestic context. In turn this has made countries less willing to take on new IMF commitments which would limit the freedom of their exchange rate policies.

The experience of managed floating since mid-1973 has led to widespread concern that exchange rate fluctuations have been excessive and have disrupted trade and investment flows. Despite substantial official intervention, the variations in exchange rates in the first two and a half years of generalised floating were, according to Williamson (1977), more pronounced than before 1973 by 'just about any standard' with daily changes of up to 4%, weekly movements approaching 10% and quarterly swings on occasion exceeding 20%. The Economist (March 1978) calculated that in the six months to March 1978 the Swiss franc appreciated on a trade weighted basis by over 20%, the Japanese yen by 8½% and the Deutschemark by just over 6%.

Movements of this magnitude have often been larger than would have been necessary to correct a balance of payments disequilibrium. The lags in external adjustment and the initial perverse effect of exchange rate changes (the J curve) have sometimes prompted expectations of further changes in the same direction; and the foreign exchange markets have simply followed the band-wagon. The resulting erratic swings have been unrelated to underlying economic conditions as was the case, for example, with the fall and rise of sterling in 1976-77.

However, the volatility of exchange rates since mid-1973 is not altogether surprising. Large fluctuations were to some extent inevitable given the uncertainties caused by the Arab oil embargo and two-figure global inflation. The hesitant recovery from the 1974-75 recession has done little to reduce divergent inflation and balance of payments trends which, as already shown, were a contributory cause of the dollar's decline over the year to mid-1978. The extent of the fluctuations should also be kept in perspective: the net changes were similar to those experienced during the major crises of the par value system in August-December 1971 and February-March 1973; and a large part of the dollar's depreciation between mid-1977 and mid-1978 was understandable in the context of its over-valuation in 1975-76 and the need to offset a relatively high US inflation rate (as compared with West Germany and Japan).

It could also be argued that the foreign exchange markets have learnt to accept floating rates. An IMF analysis (1977) covering operations in the spot and forward exchange markets in eight major currencies concluded that 'the deviations between forward exchange rates and actual spot rates at the time the forward contracts mature were smaller during 1976 than in previous years for many of the major currencies'. On this evidence — compiled before the 1977-78 fall of the dollar — it would appear that market participants were better at anticipating exchange rate movements in 1976 than in previous years and that, despite periodic upheavals, the underlying determinants of exchange rates had become less variable than in 1973-74.

Importantly, greater flexibility of exchange rates has made some contribution to the international adjustment process, in that changes in rates have been used to offset differences in inflation rates among the major countries. An IMF comparison (1977) of relative wholesale prices for manufactured goods, adjusted for effective exchange rate changes, found very little change in the pattern of competitiveness among eight leading industrial countries between early 1973 and the first quarter of 1977. Only Switzerland and Italy showed a clear change in competitive position over the period. Similar results were obtained from a survey of unit labour costs in manufacturing for this group of countries: on this index the competitive gains of Italy were larger than on the comparison above, while the United States and the United Kingdom had also moved into positions of increasing competitiveness by the start of 1977.

The IMF's conclusions have been reinforced by evidence from the OECD (July 1977) which undertook the same kind of analysis in mid-1977. In this case the OECD looked at a wider group of countries and based their findings on an average of three indicators — export prices, unit labour costs and consumer prices — over the periods 1970-73 and 1973-76. The general impression gained was that between 1973 and 1976 exchange rates in eleven selected countries moved in line with relative differences in domestic inflation. In other words, exchange rate movements in this period prevented some current account imbalances from developing or widening as a result of divergent patterns of inflation.

However, floating exchange rates have contributed only marginally to the reduction of existing current account imbalances. As explained in Chapter Four, current account developments in the major industrial countries have been governed by other factors, in particular the 1973 oil price increase and the speed with which individual governments introduced restrictive demand management policies. Empirical work by the OECD (July 1977) has shown that, while there were important changes in 'real' exchange rates between 1970 and 1973, i.e. changes which did not simply offset inflation differentials, the same did not apply in 1973-76. Except for Switzerland there was no clear cut case of a significant change — of more than 5% — in real exchange rates among OECD members since the adoption of general floating.

The limited role of exchange rate changes in establishing a sustainable payments structure can be explained by three main reasons. Firstly, external balance was not given a high priority in several countries before 1976-78 and the flexibility of exchange rates was reduced by intervention and other measures such as foreign borrowing, exchange restrictions and capital controls. Denmark, Norway, Sweden, France and the United Kingdom were examples of European countries which financed current account deficits through external borrowing in 1974-77. Secondly, trade performance since 1973 has been influenced by non-price structural factors such as a reputation for quality, reliable delivery schedules, good after-sales services and the development of new products. It would have been unrealistic to expect that unanticipated and possibly unsustained changes in relative prices, induced by exchange rate movements, would have had a rapid effect on patterns of production and demand that reflect such structural factors. At the very least traders have to ensure that relative price changes will last before they undertake the large adjustment costs involved in any shift in the pattern of demand or supply. The slowness of such adjustment may have been increased since 1974-75 by the depth of the world recession and the continued strength of inflationary expectations.

Thirdly, and perhaps most importantly, the effectiveness of exchange rate changes since 1973 has been impaired by the absence of appropriate domestic policies. In deficit countries, for example, avoidance of the so-called vicious circle of depreciation (leading to offsetting price and cost movements and further depreciation) depends in many cases on adequate restraint of domestic demand and on incomes policies of the kind used by the United Kingdom in 1976-78. It also presupposes co-operation by surplus countries in the form of demand stimulation (to encourage imports) and exchange rate appreciation. As the 1977 IMF *Annual Report* has pointed out, both demand management and exchange rate policies have essential parts, distinct but interrelated, to play in successful international adjustment. Use of one without the other has often proved ineffective in recent years.

Not surprisingly the Amended Article IV (Obligations regarding Exchange Rates) is an attempt to give the IMF much broader powers in this sphere than hitherto. The par value provisions have been replaced and in their stead members are allowed to adopt the exchange arrangements of their choice. The IMF is authorised to undertake 'firm surveillance' of these arrangements and to oversee the effective operation of the international monetary system by ensuring that members pursue orderly and responsible economic and financial policies. In contrast to the Bretton Woods system, the Fund is able to initiate consultations with members suspected of defaulting on these obligations (see below).

The Amended Article IV also allows the IMF to authorise, by an 85% majority, a return to stable but adjustable par values when international monetary developments permit. In such a case members would still be free to continue with their own exchange arrangements, but those which opted to establish par values would have to maintain the value of their currencies within agreed margins against a common denominator (probably the SDR). As under the 1944-73 system, par value changes could only be justified, with IMF concurrence, by 'fundamental disequilibrium' in the economy of the member concerned. Termination of a par value would be possible at any time, but if the IMF objected the member could become ineligible to use Fund resources.

The Amended Article IV is at least realistic. The likely persistence of large payments imbalances and of a high level of global inflation makes any more structured alternative unworkable at present. However, it is indicative of the political pressures within the Fund that it took two and a half years to reach an agreement which does not change events so much as recognise them. The Article is deliberately vague, so as to accommodate the very different views of France and the United States, and as Hirsch (1976) has pointed out it is 'a telling and not wholly reassuring sign of the times that the exchange rate provision, which has still to be regarded as the core of an international monetary order, should be so much an open book'.

If IMF surveillance of exchange rates, described by Witteveen (1976) as one of the most challenging of future IMF tasks, is to mean anything, much will depend on adherence to the Principles and Procedures adopted by the Interim Committee in April 1977 for the guidance of members' exchange rate policies. Essentially the Principles are a stronger version of the 1974 Guidelines for Floating, backed by the legal authority of Amended Article IV. In theory exchange rate management will be based on three main tenets — avoidance of exchange rate manipulation for 'unfair' competitive advantage, intervention to counter short-term 'disorder' in exchange markets and consideration of other members' interests. IMF surveillance will take the form of annual consultations which will supersede the regular Article VIII and Article XIV consultations. Appraisal of members' exchange rate policies will take place within the framework of a 'comprehensive analysis of the general economic situation and economic policy strategy of the member' covering the balance of payments, reserves and external indebtedness.

The IMF is now specifically authorised to initiate discussions with a member if there is evidence of:

   (i)   protracted one-way intervention on a large scale;
  (ii)   unsustainable levels of official borrowing or lending for balance of payments purposes;
 (iii)   prolonged maintenance of current or capital account restrictions and incentives;
  (iv)   domestic policies providing 'abnormal' encouragement or discouragement to capital flows; and
   (v)   where the behaviour of the exchange rate appears unrelated to underlying economic and financial conditions.

The Managing Director also has the power to raise difficulties informally with members. The implementation of surveillance is to be reviewed annually by the Executive Board which will also examine 'broad developments' in exchange rates at regular intervals in the context of international adjustment.

It would therefore seem that the IMF is now in a better position to ensure that flexible exchange rates contribute more to adjustment and that exchange rate appreciation or depreciation is accompanied by suitable domestic policies. However, governments are unlikely to welcome outside

interference in their economic management and are reluctant to take on new
commitments for the sake of international consistency.   The IMF is heavily
reliant on moral suasion: its sanctions are limited, with no mechanism for
calling to account countries with strongly over-valued or under-valued
currencies.   The Principles may also prove difficult to administer given
the wide range of policies which have a direct or indirect bearing on the
exchange rate.   Furthermore the definition of a disorderly market varies
over time and from country to country: and it is often impossible for
central banks and monetary authorities to distinguish in advance between
exchange rate movements which are temporary and will be reversed and those
which reflect an underlying trend.

It may thus be some time before an acceptable code of practice
based on experience can be developed by the IMF.   Initially the Fund may
need to concentrate on the extreme cases where the problems can be easily
identified.   From there the Principles may be used to identify and
encourage co-operative approaches among Fund members to exchange rate
matters.   IMF influence will probably be small on the policies of countries such as the United States, West Germany and Japan but even here the
Principles provide an agreed framework for bilateral support arrangements.

In this fashion the IMF Principles could act as a starting point
for moves towards a more structured exchange rate system than the present
ad hoc arrangements.   The medium-term prospects for a return to stable
but adjustable par values are slight despite LDC pressure, historical
precedent and the nostalgia of some central bankers.   On present economic
forecasts such a system would be subject to the same tensions experienced
from 1965 to 1973 and, to be practicable, would require internationally
agreed rules on adjustment and the control of world liquidity, which seem
less likely to be forthcoming now than at the start of the reform exercise
in 1972.   It may be more realistic to consider less ambitious target zone
proposals for major currencies, an idea which was incorporated in the
abortive 1974 Guidelines for Floating.   In mid-1978 the EEC countries
were examining Franco-German proposals for greater exchange market stability
which would involve *inter alia* linking the pound sterling, the French franc
and the Italian lira to the European 'snake' by early 1979.   On a wider
scale, target zones for the three major currencies, the dollar, the
Deutschemark and the yen, have been advocated by such influential figures
as Burns (former FRB Chairman), Roosa (former US Treasury Under Secretary)
and Cort (formerly chairman of the EEC Monetary Committee).   But the
adoption of these schemes presupposes a greater degree of current account
stability in the EEC countries, and in the United States, West Germany and
Japan, as well as agreement on appropriate reference zones.   The bickering
between the major countries over the dollar rate in the mid-1977 to mid-
1978 period is hardly an encouraging precedent.

In the future, therefore, it can be said that the potential exists
for much wider IMF supervision of exchange rate policies, but whether or
not it can be made effective will rest ultimately on the goodwill and
co-operation of IMF members, qualities which have been in short supply in
recent years.

(e) Lending conditions

The other important way in which the IMF can directly influence
adjustment policies is through its power to impose conditions on its lending.
This power is well established, generally accepted and central to the Fund's

future role, but it is also an area where IMF 'severity' has been increasingly subject to criticism, much of it misplaced.

The conditions for lending are set out only in very general terms in the pre-1978 and Amended Articles. The Amended Article V, 3 states:

> 'The Fund shall adopt policies on the use of its general resources .... and may adopt special policies for special balance of payments problems, that will assist members to solve their balance of payments problems in a manner consistent with the provisions of this Agreement and that will establish adequate safeguards for the temporary use of the general resources of the Fund.'

None of the pre-conditions for a drawing (Amended Article V, 3(b)) can be interpreted as a deterrent. A member's 'need' to draw 'because of its balance of payments or its reserve position or developments in its reserves' is determined flexibly on a case-by-case basis. Where possible the procedures are used by the IMF staff in such a way as to benefit applicants.

IMF policies have evolved gradually with experience. They are embodied in a series of Executive Board Decisions, such as the 1952 Rooth Plan outlined in Chapter One, which although not legally binding carry considerable weight. Access to IMF resources, according to a 1952 Decision, is dependent primarily on the 'temporary nature' of a member's problem. Fund lending is designed to assist members to correct balance of payments maladjustments and not to finance longer-term development needs — which is the province of the World Bank. The second important aspect is that a member's policies should be deemed adequate to overcome its problems within a reasonable period. It is 'the policies above all which should determine the Fund's attitude'. No general rules are laid down 'in view of the diversity of problems and institutional arrangements' and there is a caveat in a related 1968 Decision that lending agreements should cover only 'those performance criteria necessary to ensure the achievement of agreed objectives, but no others'.

Since July 1969, a gold tranche drawing (75%-100% of quota) has been legally automatic. The same now applies to the reserve tranche under the Amended Articles. Because of this many countries, including the United Kingdom, count the undrawn part of their gold or reserve tranche in their official reserves. All other requests for drawings are examined by the IMF to determine whether the proposed use would be consistent with the Articles and with Fund policies (see above). The criteria are more liberal when the request is in the first credit tranche (normally 100%-125% of quota) than when it is in the three higher credit tranches (normally 125%-200% of quota).

With a first credit tranche drawing, the IMF's attitude is, in the words of the 1952 Decision, 'a liberal one' provided only that 'the member ... is making reasonable efforts to solve its problems'. The IMF also takes into account factors such as general creditworthiness and previous record of repayment. Where differences arise the member is almost always given the benefit of the doubt. Drawings in the higher credit tranches are nearly always made under standby arrangements and require more substantial justification. Fund credit in these cases is often phased over one or two years and each instalment is subject to performance criteria dealing with all aspects of monetary, fiscal and trade policies. These criteria sometimes extend to government financing requirements, reserve levels and external debt.

Borrowing from the IMF is relatively cheap when compared with market finance. Before July 1974 interest charges were determined by a formula related to the amount of a drawing and the length of time such drawing was outstanding; but since then charges on ordinary tranche drawings have been set at 4% for the first year rising by ½% per annum to a maximum of 6% if the drawing is outstanding after five years. The Amended Articles state that charges will be decided by a 70% majority of the Executive Board, that they will be uniform for all members and that they will 'normally' rise over the period a drawing is outstanding. There is also provision, as previously, for service charges on each drawing, but that on reserve tranche purchases may not exceed ½%. Charges are payable in SDRs but in exceptional circumstances the Fund may permit a member to pay in the currencies of other members specified by the IMF or in the member's own currency (Amended Article V, 8).

Repurchase (i.e. repayment) of drawings under the gold or reserve tranche, as well as drawings under the credit tranches, is normally required within three to five years. Drawings under standby arrangements are designed to be repurchased in three years but such repurchases can be, and often are, rescheduled over the fourth and fifth years if the member has a continuing balance of payments need. Under the Amended Articles the complex, rigid and often inconvenient provisions for compulsory re-purchase in the event of an improvement in a member's reserves have been removed. Instead the IMF will measure the ability of a borrower to repurchase by more flexible criteria and repurchase will only be 'expected normally' as a member's 'balance of payments and reserve position improves'. There is provision, subject to high voting majorities, for the IMF to vary the repurchase period for all members and to postpone repurchase in individual cases of exceptional hardship. Repurchases must be made in SDRs or currencies specified by the Fund, in consultation with members, on the basis of their balance of payments and reserve positions, developments in the foreign exchange markets and the desirability of promoting, over time, balanced positions in the Fund (Amended Article V, 7).

Despite this apparent flexibility, Fund conditions have been increasingly attacked by deficit countries. In part this reflects what *The Economist* (4 March 1978) called 'the natural political need to offload the odium that will be brought by the painful process of economic adjust-ment required to eradicate an insupportable balance of payments deficit'; but it also reflects the feeling among LDCs and other debtors that IMF conditions are ill-adapted to their development needs. According to Abdalla (1977), the Fund 'persists in applying remedies conceived for developed countries' maladies to those of the Third World', a view publicly shared by the President of Peru after that country's dealings with the IMF in 1977-78. It has also been argued that IMF recommend-ations are over-stringent and impose drastic adjustment in an unrealistic time period. In the words of Islam (1976), the Fund has not shown 'sympathetic awareness of the political constraints on economic policy-making' or that 'the results of policy changes take more than five years'.

The fear of inappropriately severe targets is demonstrated by the general reluctance among LDCs to draw in the higher credit tranches. At end-1977 only a handful of these members, including Chile and Pakistan, had borrowed beyond the first credit tranche although the number has since increased, with large borrowings by Jamaica and Zambia. In mid-1978 none had reached the maximum (200% of quota and beyond), unlike two indus-trial countries, the United Kingdom and Italy, in 1976-77. LDC fears are strengthened by what they see as their lack of bargaining power, in contrast to a country like the United Kingdom, to persuade the IMF to compromise on terms. An exception occurred with Jamaica in 1977, but that country's lobbying was effective because it was supported by the United States and the United Kingdom and because the standby agreement was entered into by a government which could fulfil most of its commitments to the IMF. The same has not been true, until recently, of problem cases like Portugal and Turkey where weak minority governments were in no position in 1977 to agree to or to enforce any conditions.

There is some evidence to support the criticisms by LDCs and other debtors. On the technical side the IMF may have over-estimated the efficacy of devaluation as a means of reducing the volume of imports in countries such as Peru, Jamaica and Turkey where the demand for imports is relatively price-inelastic. In addition the IMF has at times appeared over-confident with regard to the ability of governments to restrain the inflationary impact of currency depreciation through domestic incomes policies. In the smaller less sophisticated economies like Zaire the IMF's traditional performance criteria — such as fixed limits on domestic credit expansion — may be largely beyond the member's control, except fortuitously. In these countries the techniques for implementing and monitoring restrictive fiscal and monetary policies are, at best, rudimentary.

Most LDCs, by their nature, have no unique criterion of disequilibrium, equivalent to a current account deficit for industrial countries. Given that their development needs are often virtually unlimited, the current balance has in practice been determined by the availability of finance from the industrial countries (before 1973) and OPEC. Although the rise in oil prices has increased the import bill for many LDCs, in some cases at least it has also led to an increase in available financing from OPEC lenders. In the not indefensible view of the governments concerned this may not, *per se*, imply a need for anything other than very gradual adjustment measures.

On the other hand these strictures ignore the fact that the Fund is normally well aware of the limits imposed on national governments by domestic social and political considerations. Fund procedures depend on consultation and co-operation and the IMF staff often assists members with the required economic and financial analysis and forecasting. Although the failure to meet particular targets can temporarily deprive a member of further IMF credit — as in the case of Peru in March 1978 — it is possible to retain access if additional measures can be agreed to achieve previous targets. This was true of Jamaica in February 1978.

A real attempt is made by the staff to adapt stabilisation measures to the causes of individual problems and to different institutional structures. Lending transactions in 1975-78 show wide differences in performance criteria applied to borrowers, even in the higher credit tranches, let alone the more nebulous area of the first credit tranche. Conditions attached to the UK and Italian loans in 1976-77 were much more detailed and more complex, involving quarterly monitoring of domestic credit expansion and public sector borrowing targets, than those for LDC borrowers such as Burma and the Sudan.

If a certain sameness is apparent in the IMF's 1977-78 austerity packages for Peru, Zambia and Zaire it is largely because the problems of these countries, and their causes, are also similar. In each case the authorities were slow to react to the 1974-75 world recession and the collapse of the boom in commodity prices; and in each case the IMF was faced with record current account deficits accompanied by very low growth, high unemployment and two-figure inflation.

(f) *Special facilities*

Moreover, the IMF has considerably modified the conditions of its lending in response to the magnitude and apparent intractability of payments' imbalances since 1973-74. New facilities have been set up and existing ones liberalised to the particular benefit of LDCs. The relatively light conditions have prompted a heavy concentration of drawings in these facilities which has radically changed the form of IMF credit over the last decade. This can be seen in the following table.

Table 6.2   The form of IMF credit, end 1973-77

SDR million

	1973	1974	1975	1976	1977[1]
Credit tranches	554	1,484	1,949	3,166	3,866
Oil facility	-	1,716	4,759	6,702	6,530
Compensatory finance	460	535	718	2,713	2,767
Other[2]	14	5	12	98	238
Total	1,028	3,740	7,438	12,678	13,400

Source: IMF, *Annual Reports*

[1] October

[2] From December 1973-July 1975 buffer stock only: from August 1975-August 1976 buffer stock and extended facility: from September 1976 extended facility only

The oil facility was established in mid-1974 and renewed in 1975 to help IMF members meet the impact on their balance of payments of the increase in oil prices. It was not financed from the general resources of the IMF but by borrowings from the oil producers and other surplus countries. Conditions were minimal in 1974 with the borrower promising not to introduce current account restrictions and also outlining policies on energy conservation and on achieving balance of payments equilibrium in the medium term. Conditions were slightly stricter in 1975 but only the equivalent of those for a first credit tranche drawing. Borrowers agreed to take 'reasonable' steps towards a sustainable external position over an 'appropriate' period. In nearly all cases the IMF allowed borrowers considerable leeway when the letters of intent were drawn up. The low degree of conditionality is shown by the high proportion of eligible countries that utilised the facility. Between September 1974 and May 1976 56 members borrowed a total of SDR 6.9 billion.

Although the facility is no longer available it did provide virtually unconditional finance on reasonably generous terms, including repayment over four to seven years and an interest subsidy for 18 of the poorest LDC borrowers, designed to reduce the interest rate on their oil facility loans from 7.71% to 2.71% per annum. The facility was an important indirect link between OPEC and oil-importing countries and helped the latter to avoid precipitate adjustment via deflation or trade controls which would have intensified the 1974-75 recession. It also demonstrated the IMF's adaptability and its awareness of LDC problems.

On the other hand, despite the attraction of market-related interest rates, the IMF was handicapped firstly by OPEC reluctance to contribute because of their limited influence and interest in Fund operations and secondly by the industrial countries' doubts over the appropriateness of this kind of lending by the Fund. Total contributions of just under SDR 7 billion from 17 lenders were very small in comparison with the 1974-75 OPEC surplus and the oil-related deficit of other countries. At the same time the very light conditions were widely ignored and had only a marginal effect on borrowers' attitude to adjustment.

The 'extended fund facility' (EFF) was established in September 1974 to provide balance of payments assistance, basically for LDCs, in larger amounts (up to 140% of quota) and for longer periods (three to eight years) than under conventional tranche policies. Assistance is aimed at countries in 'special circumstances of balance of payments difficulty' where there are structural maladjustments or inherently slow growth rates. The decision setting up the facility requires applicants to present a programme adequate for the solution of the member's problem covering the whole period of the extended arrangement and a detailed statement of policies for the first year, with the understanding that the member will supply similar statements for subsequent years. Drawings are phased in instalments over the first three years of the arrangement, subject to performance criteria concentrating on mobilising existing resources and lessening reliance on external restrictions.

The conditions are therefore quite strict — considerably more so than for drawings in the first credit tranche. However, they are in keeping with the larger amounts and longer time scale of the EFF and are marginally less stringent than for higher credit tranche drawings. The facility seems particularly suited to the longer-term problems now faced by many LDCs; and the IMF staff have already had an important role in drawing up programmes tailored to individual countries' needs.

Less optimistically the future development of the EFF is the subject of controversy within the Fund. According to the industrial countries, and the IMF staff, the facility is designed to be used by three or four least developed countries a year and each borrower should have a comprehensive and realistic programme to put things right. The LDCs argue that the EFF should be open to any country with a structural imbalance and a development plan, however vague and impracticable. They have pressed for larger amounts to be made available and relaxation of the conditions which they see as a major disincentive to use. Liberalisation of this facility has been advocated by Islam (1976), as an appropriate response to the 'adverse turn in external economic developments' which have aggravated LDC adjustment problems since 1973-74.

Such criticisms ignore the IMF's traditionally flexible approach which takes full account of existing development plans. The real deterrent to use is the reluctance of most LDCs to take on any far-reaching commitments in an uncertain economic climate, particularly since the

amounts they can borrow under this facility, though large in an IMF context, are small in relation to their longer-term needs.   At end-March
1978 only three countries, Kenya, Mexico and the Philippines, had agreed
arrangements, for a combined total of SDR 800 million.   The lack of
enthusiasm of both IMF creditors and debtors seems likely to restrict
future EFF drawings except perhaps in conjunction with the new supplementary financing facility.

        Perhaps the most extreme example of the new IMF approach to
lending conditions is the 'trust fund' which is specifically designed to
provide concessional assistance to 61 eligible developing countries between
mid-1976 and mid-1980.   Finance will come from the profits on the sale of
one-sixth (25 million ounces) of the IMF's gold, as agreed by the Interim
Committee in August 1975 and explained in more detail in Chapter Three.
Borrowers have only to demonstrate a 'need' for balance of payments
assistance, which is liberally interpreted, together with 'reasonable'
efforts to remedy its external position.   These are met if the IMF has
already approved a stabilisation programme under a standby or extended
arrangement, otherwise access is subject to first credit tranche criteria.
The terms are also generous.   The interest cost is only ½% per annum and
loans are repayable over five years, which works out at an effective
grant element of 49%.   There is provision for rescheduling in cases of
serious hardship and a review clause implicitly allows for the conversion
of some trust fund loans into grants.

        The major weakness of the trust fund is that the amounts involved
are derisory in comparison with the financing requirements of LDCs.   Despite high prices in the 1978 IMF gold auctions, the cumulative profits
totalled only some $1.5 billion in mid-April 1978, with twelve million
ounces sold.   The three 'interim disbursements' since early 1977 amounted
to just $0.4 billion, half of which went to five countries — Pakistan,
Egypt, the Philippines, Thailand and Bangladesh.   Assuming that gold
sales are continued until mid-1980 at an average of $140 per ounce — a
profit of $100 — the overall yield will be somewhere between $2.5-3.0
billion.   But only three-quarters of these profits will go to the trust
fund; the rest is being distributed to a wider group of LDCs in proportion to their share in IMF quotas at end-August 1975.   (Some $0.1 billion
was distributed in this way after the 1976 auctions.)   Although the OPEC
countries are donating their share to the trust fund, several middle-
income LDCs have not yet done so; and voluntary contributions to the fund
from developed countries have also fallen well short of original hopes.
At most the trust fund should be able to lend some $0.75 billion in each
of the three years 1978 to 1980.

        Not surprisingly the trust fund is regarded as totally inadequate
by LDCs.   It is also viewed with suspicion by IMF creditors because, in
the words of Roosa (1976), it has moved the Fund 'dangerously' close
to the zone reserved for the IBRD' and 'may tear a gaping hole in the
fabric of the institution that is supposed to ensure the integrity of the
world monetary system'.   The fears may be exaggerated but it is true that
aid-related operations could weaken the confidence of powerful countries
in the IMF who look to it as a source of payments discipline on deficit
members.   The Fund is certainly not equipped nor designed to handle aid
transfers, particularly on the scale desired by LDCs.

        The 'compensatory finance facility' (CFF) was set up in 1963 to
assist members, particularly primary producers, experiencing temporary
shortfalls in export receipts.   Access criteria are liberal, similar to

the first credit tranche. A member has to demonstrate, in accordance with an agreed formula, that the shortfall is both temporary and beyond the member's control. After this, drawings, up to a uniform percentage of quota over and above ordinary tranche drawings, are almost uncondi- tional in that the member has only a general obligation to 'co-operate' in finding 'appropriate' solutions to its payments difficulties.

Before December 1975 drawings were kept to a low level by rela- tively modest quota limits on borrowing and conservative application of the formula which determined the extent of a shortfall and consequent entitlement to compensatory finance. Although the philosophy of the facility has not been changed since then, important operational decisions have substantially increased the amounts available. The previous upper limit on forecasts of export earnings in the shortfall formula has been replaced by a calculation based on past trends, subject only to 'judge- mental appraisal' by the Fund and the member. The limit on drawings has been raised to 50% of quota in any twelve months and 75% for outstanding drawings which allows IMF assistance to cover a greater part of the cal- culated shortfall. More timely compensation is also available through an early drawing procedure based on estimated data.

The moves towards greater liberalisation coincided with primary exporters' urgent need for compensatory finance after the collapse of world commodity prices in 1975-76. In the period February 1976 to January 1977, SDR 2.35 billion was drawn from the CFF by 48 countries whose export earnings, on average, were 13% lower in the shortfall year than in the preceding year. This was double total purchases in the CFF's previous 13-year existence and almost double total credit tranche drawings in 1976. At end-October 1977 outstanding purchases were a record SDR 2.77 billion.

The changes again show the IMF's adaptability, which enabled the CFF to make a useful contribution towards alleviating the instability of world commodity markets in 1976. However, several borrowers want further liberalisation in the form of easier conditions and more compensation. In 1977 proposals were made in the IMF Executive Board for a minimum compen- sation limit, related not to quota but to the extent of a shortfall, and for repayment to be dependent on the subsequent recovery in export earnings. It was also suggested that compensation to least developed countries should be in the form of grants.

These demands can be traced to the failure of other United Nations commodity initiatives outlined in Chapter Seven. They reflect misunder- standing of the CFF's role as a source of finance to meet temporary prob- lems rather than to provide longer-term aid or concessional financing. A further increase in the amounts available would add to the strains on IMF liquidity without a commensurate contribution to adjustment, since several members have succeeded in using the CFF as an alternative to the more con- ditional finance in the upper credit tranches. It seems improbable that IMF creditors will permit a second overhaul of the CFF in the near future. Drawings fell considerably in 1977 and there is unlikely to be a major surge in 1978-80 if the recovery in world trade is maintained. Assuming that it is two to three years before the Seventh General Quota Review — dis- cussed in Chapter Seven — is implemented, the CFF will remain a limited source of adjustment finance in the medium term.

The 'buffer stock facility' (BSF) was established in 1969 to assist in financing members' contributions to international buffer stock arrangements for various commodities which meet certain agreed criteria. Drawings under the BSF are conditional only on the borrower's 'need' and on 'co-operation' with the IMF to deal with payments problems. Originally drawings were subject to a joint 75% of quota limit with compensatory finance drawings, but this has not applied since December 1975. Drawings are now permitted up to 50% of quota and, under the Amended Articles, no longer affect a member's ordinary tranche position. In this respect the BSF is now similar to the CFF.

However, only SDR 30 million has been drawn from the BSF in the past nine years and there were no outstanding drawings at end-1977. Its contribution to conditional liquidity is unlikely to be substantially increased by the widening of the facility in December 1977 to cover, not just cash contributions to internationally owned buffer stocks, but the financing of national buffer stocks under international supervision. Drawings were permitted to finance IMF members' stocks under the 1977 International Sugar Agreement, aimed at stabilising world sugar prices and signatories' export earnings. The benefits of this will be restricted to a small group of sugar-producing countries.

1976 and beyond

From the above it can be seen that much of IMF credit granted between 1974 and 1977 was effectively unconditional. In 1975, for instance, about 90% of Fund drawings did not commit borrowers to specific targets or to anything more binding than general statements on future economic policy. This would imply that LDC criticisms of the IMF as a financial dictator wedded to austerity are not really justified. Indeed the IMF has been very quick to adapt its lending to the particular problems of its poorer members in the 1970s.

Since 1976-77, however, the emphasis in the IMF has (rightly) reverted from financing to adjustment. The IMF staff and the major creditor countries have become increasingly aware of the dangers of a situation where unprecedented current account deficits have been financed by massive external borrowing, mainly from commercial banks. The IMF is in a position, through the mechanism of conditional financial support and surveillance of economic policy and management, to encourage the kind of orderly but forceful adjustment programme that may be necessary to permit the restoration of balance of payments equilibrium. Although adjustment is not an easy option politically, the experience of the IMF in 1977 with countries as diverse as the United Kingdom and Mexico shows that appropriate adjustment policies need not be detrimental to growth and employment and can provide an essential basis for healthier and more sustained economic development.

Looking to the future two factors are particularly important. Firstly, the absence of agreement on how the adjustment process should be working, and what its aims should be, means that IMF conditions will have to be applied, as now, on a case-by-case basis — an extension of the Fund's traditionally flexible approach. This does not imply that conditions should now be relaxed but that the IMF should recognise, in its credit tranche lending, the exceptional nature of the present imbalance and that it cannot be eliminated in the short term without economic and social disruption. IMF conditions should therefore be directed to a slower pace of adjustment and perhaps be applied over a longer period than

hitherto.   There are signs, notably in the introduction of two-year
(formerly one-year) standby programmes and in the conditions attached to
drawings under the extended fund facility and the supplementary financing
facility that the Fund may be moving in this direction.

Secondly, the IMF's influence on members' policies will depend
to a large extent on whether or not members think it worth their while,
in respect of the conditions, to borrow from the Fund.   Seen in isola-
tion the IMF has considerably expanded its financing role since 1973 but
the various initiatives have provided only a very small proportion of
borrowers' overall needs.   The IMF has been used as the lender of last
resort and Morgan Guaranty (April 1977) estimated that only 8-9% ($14
billion) of the $200 billion global imbalance between 1974 and 1977 was
financed by Fund credit.   To date, action by the IMF on the necessary
scale has been prevented by the conflicting interests of debtor and
creditor countries but, if the Fund were able to lend in larger amounts
than hitherto, it is possible that its conditions would become more
acceptable to potential borrowers.   In the words of Witteveen (1977)
'to be effective in influencing the speed and nature of members' adjustment, the share of international liquidity provided by the IMF must be
substantial in relation to the size of members' payments problems'.   To
increase its influence the Fund must first increase its resources.

CHAPTER SEVEN

FINANCING AND THE IMF 1973-78

As explained in the previous chapter, the measures taken by the IMF to expand its lending, such as the establishment of the oil facility, the trust fund and the EFF, and the liberalisation of the CFF and BSF, have had little impact on members' financing needs. On the other hand the IMF measures have put a severe strain on its liquidity and this chapter examines the need to increase IMF resources and possible ways of doing so.

The position at end-1977

The record use of the Fund's special facilities since 1974, made without a corresponding increase in members' contributions to the IMF, has led to a marked decline in its holdings of usable currencies (those currencies which can be used in IMF operations because of the issuers' balance of payments and reserve strength). Although the number of usable currencies doubled between mid-1976 and early 1978 the effect has been limited since most are usable only in small amounts (even Saudi Arabian rials) while the position of several creditors weakened sharply over this period. Just over half the October 1977 total of usable currencies, some SDR 6.0 billion, was US dollars and eighty per cent comprised the currencies of nine members — Brazil, Canada, Denmark, West Germany, Japan, Netherlands, Indonesia, Malaysia and the United States — some of whom already had a high proportion of official reserves in the form of reserve positions in the IMF.

The strain on Fund resources was particularly evident in late 1976 and early 1977 in the financing arrangements made to accommodate the UK and Italian loan applications. Participants in the GAB were asked to provide the bulk of the finance, since the IMF could only provide SDR 500 million (14.9% of the proposed UK drawing) and SDR 75 million (16.7% of the Italian drawing) respectively from its ordinary resources. These proportions were much lower than the share of industrial country drawings financed directly by the Fund in the 1960s. Despite an improvement in the Fund's liquidity since early 1977, partly as a result of the substantial strengthening in the economic position of the United Kingdom, the ratio of IMF usable assets (currencies and SDRs) to liabilities has remained at a historically low level since mid-1975. At end-October 1977 usable assets totalled just over SDR 7.0 billion, compared with SDR 10.0 billion in April 1975, against liabilities of some SDR 18.5 billion, including loan claims under the oil facility and the GAB. In early 1978 the weakness of the dollar, on which the IMF is heavily dependent, further jeopardised the Fund's ability to lend.

Without a major extension of resources it is difficult to see how the IMF will be in a position to react flexibly to any new crisis in the world economy.   The small size of its operations will mean, as now, that countries will find it anomalous to submit to comprehensive credit conditions.   In the opinion of Kafka (1976), then IMF Executive Director for Latin America, the Fund may be left in a peripheral role as 'pawnbroker to the poorest or most mismanaged economies'.   An overhaul of IMF facilities is made more urgent by the inadequacy of other international organisations' financing arrangements and the failure of recent initiatives on aid, debt and commodities outlined below.

Non-IMF moves

As already explained in Chapter Six the OECD has an important role in co-ordinating the economic policies of the major industrial countries. However, the OECD has been unable to reinforce its influence with effective financing facilities.   The best example was the abortive 'financial support fund' (FSF) which was inspired by the US authorities in response to the 1973 oil price rise.   It was intended as an SDR 20 billion supplement to, not replacement of, other channels of official finance, which would operate for a two-year period.   Members' contributions and voting power would be determined by their FSF quotas which would be based on relative levels of GNP and foreign trade.   Finance was to be provided through direct country contributions or through individual countries agreeing to underwrite market borrowing by the FSF.   Alternatively the FSF would be authorised to borrow in national or international markets on the collective guarantee of participants.   Countries could be exempted for balance of payments reasons from contributing to a particular loan by a two-thirds majority of the governing board.

The FSF was designed very much as a last resort source of finance. To be eligible, borrowers would have to demonstrate serious external financing difficulties, fullest appropriate use of reserves and other multilateral facilities (including IMF credit tranches) and 'best efforts' to obtain capital on reasonable terms from other sources.   Access would be subject to rigorous conditions.   Borrowers would have to avoid current account restrictions and implement adequate balance of payments and energy policies.   Loans, at market-related interest rates for a maximum of seven years, would have to be approved by high voting majorities in the governing board and would be paid in instalments depending on satisfactory economic performance.

Although the FSF has been ratified by 16 OECD members it has never been used.   Its effective operation is dependent on US participation which has been vetoed by Congress.   In the late 1970s it might have several drawbacks, not least its apparent anti-OPEC stance and its over-reliance on market borrowing.   By definition it would be restricted to OECD members and would do nothing to assist LDCs.   The OECD, unlike the IMF, has no experience in raising money, administering conditions or ensuring repayments, which could deter market lenders.   The proposed conditions would be over-stringent and politically unacceptable in many cases, particularly by the smaller OECD countries which might be unwilling to use their IMF tranches, as required, before receiving an FSF loan.   The two-year statutory term of the facility ignores the longer-term nature of the present imbalance in international payments.   The new IMF supplementary financing facility should mark the demise of the FSF and leave the burden of multilateral payments financing to the IMF.

On a smaller scale the EEC has a similar, and useful, role to
that of the OECD in providing the forum for detailed discussion of fiscal,
monetary and exchange rate policies.   But its financing mechanisms are
by definition limited in scope to EEC members and the relatively small
amounts have not prevented Italy and the United Kingdom from making heavy
demands on the IMF and the banks since 1974.   The EEC has little experience or authority with regard to conditions, which have had only a marginal
effect on borrowers' policies.

There are three main facilities.   The short-term monetary support
arrangement (the *soutien*) is a smaller version of the Federal Reserve's
$22 billion swap network.   The total amount available is EMUA 6,950
million ($8.4 billion) and individual countries can draw up to a maximum
of their 'debtor quotas' plus some additional finance (the *rallonge*).   The
interest cost is related to market rates in the country whose currency is
borrowed (EEC currencies or dollars) and the borrower is required to
'consult' the EEC Monetary Committee on its economic position.   But loans
are designed only to counter short-term monetary disturbances and are
normally for three to six months.   The facility has only been used once,
by Italy in 1974, and although it is proposed to increase the amounts
available in 1979 the *soutien* is not intended to underpin medium-term
adjustment programmes.

A medium-term credit facility was established by the EEC in 1971.
Members' quotas total EMUA 5,450 million ($6.6 billion), after a large
increase in January 1978, and in theory the amount which an individual
country may draw is the total less its own quota.   In practice, however,
the EEC would not use the whole of the facility in this way, since it
would leave nothing for other potential borrowers for a period of two to
five years — the length of time a drawing may be outstanding.   The cost
of borrowing is higher than from the IMF and loans are subject to conditions
laid down by the EEC Monetary Committee.   So far Italy is, again, the only
borrower.   In December 1974 EMUA 1,159 million ($1.4 billion) was lent for
four years at an annual interest rate of just over 7½%.   The loan, which
was used in part to refinance an earlier *soutien* drawing, was conditional
on an agreed economic programme to reduce Italy's exceptionally high payments deficit and inflation rate.   The 1975-76 targets for public sector
expenditure and domestic credit expansion were, however, considerably
exceeded.

In 1975 the EEC also introduced its own oil facility in the form
of a joint Community borrowing scheme.   This facility is, however, very
limited in size — to a maximum of $3 billion (capital plus interest) —
and has been largely used up by two borrowers, Ireland and Italy.   The
loans of $0.3 billion and $1 billion respectively were at market rates and
subject to conditions which the EEC has not been able to enforce.   In
fact, none of the EEC facilities has had more than a very limited impact
on borrowers' needs and on their adjustment strategies.

The IBRD, like the IMF, has attempted to expand its operations
— in the sphere of development assistance and project aid — to deal with
increasing needs.   As set out in its 1977 Annual Report, the IBRD made
firm loan commitments in the financial year (FY) to April 1977 of $5.8
billion compared with $1.6 billion in FY 1970:   loans actually disbursed
totalled $2.6 billion (FY 1970 $0.8 billion).   The corresponding figures
for the International Development Association (IDA), the IBRD's 'soft'
loan agency, were commitments of $1.3 billion (FY 1970 $0.6 billion) and
disbursements of $1.3 billion (FY 1970 $0.1 billion).   Indeed, from mid-
1972 to mid-1977 IDA disbursements ($5 billion) were four times as large

as in the previous five financial years.   But the figures obscure the
effects of inflation on the two organisations.   When measured in 1976
dollars IBRD and IDA loan commitments in FY 1977 were actually lower, by
just under 1%, than in the previous year.

New ventures are subject to similar constraints as those of the
IMF.   Increases in IBRD capital involve considerable political bargaining
and delays and the Bank's Articles limit the volume of disbursed loans to
the total of 'free' capital and reserves.   Although an $8.4 billion
capital increase took effect in May 1977 it will only be sufficient for
the IBRD to sustain a reasonable volume of lending ($6-7 billion per annum)
for the period to end-1979.   The time required for the preparation of loan
projects by the IBRD and the inevitable lag between loans being committed
and being disbursed will make it impossible for the IBRD to fill any gaps
in commercial bank lending over the next two to three years.

IBRD expansion through market borrowing, its largest source of
finance, is limited by the need to keep its reputation on the international markets, a factor which also restricts the activities of regional
development banks.   Market borrowing by the IBRD has reached record levels
for four consecutive years and the gross proceeds in FY 1972 to FY 1977
($15.6 billion) were four and a half times the amount raised in the five
preceding financial years.   Not surprisingly both West Germany and the
United States, on whose capital markets the bulk of IBRD borrowing is
carried out, have shown signs of disquiet over this ambitious programme.

It is also unlikely that soft loan funds will match growing LDC
needs.   The funds available under the so-called Fourth Replenishment of
IDA, agreed in 1973, were used up by mid-1977 and currency fluctuations
reduced the amounts actually lent by $0.4 billion below the total origin-
ally pledged ($4.5 billion).   The Fifth Replenishment of $7.6 billion to
cover the period mid-1977 to mid-1980 was agreed only after a year of
negotiation;   and legislative delays in several countries made it necessary to have a temporary bridging arrangement for 1977-78 financing.

Similarly IBRD and IDA programme lending (i.e. medium-term loans
not covering specific development projects) has fallen as a proportion of
their total lending since 1974-75.   Although favoured by LDCs as a flexible response to their post oil crisis needs, the IBRD has been restrained
by its Articles which only permit such loans in 'special circumstances'.
This has been interpreted more narrowly after 1977 at the insistence of
powerful donors, such as West Germany, who are unwilling to see the IBRD
move too far away from its primary role as lender for specific development
projects.   There is scope here for much closer IBRD-IMF co-operation
whereby programme loans, based on an approved development strategy, could
be combined with medium-term adjustment finance from the IMF, possibly
from the extended fund facility.   However, co-operation between the two
institutions has not been particularly effective in the past and it would
be unrealistic to expect a great improvement under existing procedures.

As yet the hopes in the early 1970s for a 'new world economic
order' under UN auspices have not been translated into practical terms.
On the positive side OECD countries have agreed, in March 1978, to write
off their official debts to 29 of the poorest LDCs (MSAs) by turning outstanding loans into grants.   Nevertheless little has been done to improve
the present *ad hoc* arrangements for debt relief and the developed countries'
pledge, in May 1976, to give 'quick and constructive' consideration 'within
a multilateral framework' to individual requests has already been severely

tested in countries like North Korea, Peru and Turkey.   Proposals in 1977 by Waldheim, UN Secretary-General, and Corea, UNCTAD Secretary-General, for a new agency to fund LDC debt repayments have not received much support from aid-donors in the light of likely political and administrative difficulties.

        Progress has also been very slow towards an Integrated Programme for Commodities (IPC) currently being considered in the United Nations Conference on Trade and Development (UNCTAD).   The main IPC objectives include the establishment of a 'common fund' to finance a network of inter-nationally held buffer stocks of 18 agreed commodities such as sugar, copper and bauxite.   As originally conceived in 1974-75 the common fund would be used to buy these commodities if prices fell below a certain floor level and sell them if prices rose above a predetermined ceiling. In theory the common fund would be more creditworthy than a series of smaller, separate funds because investment (and risk) would be widely spread in several commodities: surpluses from one would offset deficits from another.   The buffer stock agreements for individual commodities (ICAs) would be negotiated separately and would operate with the aim of stabilising prices around their longer-term market equilibrium.

        Two negotiating conferences in 1977 failed to produce agreement on the details of the common fund, a failure which has led to continuing pressure to make larger amounts available from the IMF compensatory finance facility, as outlined in Chapter Six.   Controversial issues still outstand-ing include the method of financing the common fund (with most developed countries opposed to heavy new commitments), the distribution of voting power on the governing council and the LDC demand for a 'second window' which would finance non-stocking projects such as longer-term commodity diversification programmes.   Discussions on individual commodity agree-ments are still at the preparatory stage and are hampered by developed countries' fears of 'unrealistic' price targets.   It is therefore diffi-cult to envisage the introduction of comprehensive commodity arrangements for some time which, as already implied, will expose the IMF, particularly the special facilities, to heavy future demands.

        In sum the IMF will have to bear a very large share of the burden of official financing in the next three to four years.   The scope for expansion in other organisations to complement IMF moves is restricted by lack of expertise and a combination of political and administrative diffi-culties.   As shown below, the latter problems are shared to some extent by the IMF.

Possible IMF reforms

        On a fairly limited scale the Amended Articles provide the Fund with a more workable basis for its financing operations.   A number of procedures have been simplified and the range of possible transactions has widened.

        Amended Article V, 3 authorises the Fund to select currencies for use in drawings on the basis of principles which take into account members' balance of payments and reserve positions, developments in the exchange markets and the desirability of promoting, over time, balanced positions in the Fund.   These criteria, previously excluded from the Articles, have evolved with experience and should give the Fund a flexible operating base. Amended Article V, 3 also gives expression, in the form of another obligation on members, to a practice which previously relied on informal collaboration. In order to make all currencies held by the Fund usable in purchases, the Amended Article ensures that a member drawing a currency that is not one of a narrowly defined group of 'freely usable' currencies (those which are widely used in international payments and widely traded on exchange markets) will be able to obtain a currency of this group by an official exchange at agreed rates with the issuer of the currency originally drawn. Borrowing countries now have greater assurance of ultimately obtaining the currency of their choice.

In similar fashion all currencies held by the IMF will be usable in repurchases (Amended Article V, 7). The criteria for repurchase have been made more flexible (as explained in Chapter Six) which might accelerate the level of repayments and ease, albeit marginally, existing pressures on Fund liquidity. The decline of SDR 90 million in the level of repurchases (to SDR 870 million) in FY 1977 could be reversed in 1978-80 as oil facility drawings fall due for repayment.

Amended Article XII, 6 allows the IMF to establish an Investment Account within the new General Department by a simple majority vote in the Executive Board. The previous IMF investment programme in 1957-72 had to be based on a complicated interpretation of the Articles and had to be confined to the proceeds of gold sales because investment of the Fund's currency holdings might have affected the rights and obligations of members. The aim of the new provision is to establish a simpler and more effective means of financing IMF budget deficits which have been a regular feature of Fund operations since FY 1972.

If established, the Investment Account will be legally separate from the General Resources Account and its assets will not be usable in other IMF operations. The assets which may be invested include the profits from the sale of the remaining two-thirds of the IMF's gold which may be transferred to the Investment Account by an 85% majority in the Executive Board and currencies transferred from the General Resources Account by a 70% Executive Board majority for immediate investment. Investments will only be allowed in income-producing and marketable obligations of international financial organisations, such as the World Bank, or of members whose currencies are used for investment. No investment will be possible without the consent of the member whose currency is invested. Investment income will be held, reinvested or used to meet the Fund's current expenses — operational and administrative.

However, a final decision has not been taken on setting up the account and even if it is established its impact on Fund liquidity will be small. Transfers to the new account will require high voting majorities and will not be permitted to exceed the amount of the IMF's reserves at the time of the decision (SDR 690 million at end-April 1977). The details of any investment programme may be controversial not least because members may be reluctant, for fear of new commitments and exchange risk problems, to allow IMF investment in their domestic currency obligations. Finally any proceeds of investment can only be used to meet Fund expenses and not to supplement its lending activities.

There is also more chance under the Amended Articles that the IMF will be able to borrow on international and national financial markets. This has been advocated by Solomon (1978) and other commentators, who argue that the Fund should itself absorb some of the proceeds of the surpluses of OPEC and industrial countries and pass them on to countries

in deficit.   The possibility was rejected at the time of the 1974-75 oil
facility for practical as much as legal reasons, not least the unwillingness of private lenders to accept claims on the IMF denominated in SDRs,
which would have created problems with regard to matching their assets and
liabilities.   Two other potential drawbacks in 1974-75 concerned the Fund's
obligation to maintain the value of its currency holdings in terms of gold
(pre-1978 Article IV, 8), which would have made the Fund vulnerable to
exchange risks on the proceeds of its borrowing, and the limited scope for
the Fund to replenish 'scarce' currency holdings under the pre-1978
Article VII.

        The Amended Articles provide for all Fund assets to be kept in
the General Department or the SDR Department and all operations must be
conducted through one of these two departments (Amended Article XVI, 1).
However, it is now possible to distinguish between different accounts
within the General Department and maintenance of value will only apply to
currencies held in the General Resources Account (Amended Article V, 11).
A separate account could be established to hold and disburse funds raised
in the market under Amended Article V, 2 which states: 'If requested the
Fund may decide to perform financial and technical services, including
administration of resources contributed to by members, that are consistent
with the purposes of the Fund'.   At the same time the IMF will have more
scope for replenishment (i.e. borrowing) because the 'normal' level of
members' currency positions in the Fund (the level up to which the IMF can
legitimately replenish its holdings) will be raised gradually from 75% to
100% of quota (Amended Article V, 9).

        On the other hand a separate account for market borrowing might be
ruled out by a narrow interpretation of the Amended Introductory Article
which mentions only three accounts — General Resources, Special Disbursement and Investment — in the General Department, as outlined in Chapter
One.   Moreover the awkwardness of SDR-denominated lending for private
institutions has not been removed.   Equally, IMF market borrowing would
almost certainly be opposed in the US Congress and other legislatures as
a 'bail-out' of the banks, who would be able to transfer their international
lending risks to the Fund in exchange for a first-class investment.   IMF
borrowing might also crowd out some country borrowers.   It might be argued
that this is exactly what is needed and that high-risk countries would be
pushed out of the market and into the Fund, but there is no guarantee that
these countries would always be the ones that most needed to be subjected
to the discipline of Fund conditions.

        As already explained in Chapter Three, the Amended Articles
provide for a reduction in the role of gold as a monetary asset and its
replacement by the SDR in a wide range of IMF transactions.   In August
1975 the Interim Committee also decided that one-sixth of the IMF's gold
holdings would be sold for the benefit of developing countries through a
trust fund; and a further one-sixth would be returned to members in proportion to their quotas at end-August 1975.   In the latter case 'restitu-
tion', as it is called, is planned by the IMF in four annual instalments
from January 1977 to January 1980.   It was included in the 1975 gold
arrangements to placate the French, and the principle has been widely
condemned as giving rise to a highly arbitrary distribution of new liquidity at the expense of countries with relatively small IMF quotas.

        In theory, Amended Article V, 12 gives the Fund a wide range of
powers with respect to the remaining two-thirds of its gold holdings.   The
Fund is authorised to sell gold to members both at the present official

price and at market-related prices.   The profits will be held separately from other IMF resources in a new Special Disbursement Account and may be employed in several ways including transfers to the Investment Account and to the General Resources Account for immediate use in IMF operations. One possible use would involve a general increase in IMF quotas in proportion to members' relative shares at end-August 1975.   Alternatively the profits could be transferred to the General Resources Account 'for operations and transactions' that are not specifically authorised in the Amended Articles but are 'consistent with the purposes of the Fund'. Under this provision, balance of payments assistance might be made available 'on special terms' to developing countries 'in difficult circumstances' or the Fund might decide to distribute a portion of Special Disbursement Account assets directly to LDCs on the basis of August 1975 quotas.

The new provisions are potentially important from the viewpoint of expanding Fund resources, but their implementation depends on high voting majorities in both the Executive Board and the Board of Governors and presupposes a degree of unanimity over the future of gold as a monetary asset that simply does not exist.   Any IMF moves will inevitably be tentative, piecemeal and time-consuming given the uncertainties surrounding the free market gold price and the possible disposal and valuation of national gold holdings.   Like the trust fund any profits from future IMF sales are unlikely to keep pace with more than a small fraction of developing country needs.

New initiatives

The Amended Articles do not appear to provide the IMF with the necessary scope for increasing its resources in the medium-term future. More fundamental changes are required involving a new facility, the GAB, quotas and an SDR allocation.   Even here, the chances of resources being made available to the IMF on a scale adequate to deal with prospective demands are not high.

(a)   The supplementary financing facility

One important initiative is already under way.   In August 1977 it was agreed that the IMF should establish a 'supplementary financing facility' (SFF) and a total of SDR 8.75 billion ($11 billion) has so far been pledged by industrial countries (SDR 4.5 billion), oil producers (SDR 4.2 billion) and Guatemala (SDR 0.03 billion), as shown in Table 7.1.

The new facility will come into effect as soon as credit lines of at least SDR 7.75 billion have been legally agreed between the IMF and prospective lenders, with a minimum of six firm contributions of at least SDR 0.5 billion each.   Interest on contributions will be paid by the IMF at market-related rates, adjusted every six months in line with the rate for five year US Treasury notes.   Claims on the SFF, denominated in SDRs, will be encashable by contributors in the event of balance of payments need (interpreted very widely to the contributors' benefit).   As under the GAB, loan claims on the IMF will also be transferable between contributors, which should protect the Fund's liquidity if any one contributor wishes to opt out.

Borrowing under the SFF will be open to all IMF members experiencing balance of payments difficulties which are 'large' in relation to quota.

Table 7.1   Proposed commitments to the SFF

SDR billion

Industrial countries		
Belgium		0.15
Canada		0.2
West Germany		1.05
Japan		0.9
Netherlands		0.1
Swiss National Bank		0.65
United States		1.45
	Total	4.50
OPEC countries		
Iran		0.685
Saudi Arabia		2.15
Qatar		0.1
Venezuela		0.5
Abu Dhabi		0.15
Kuwait		0.4
Nigeria		0.22
	Total	4.205
Guatemala		0.03

Source: IMF Interim Committee Communiqué, 30 April 1978

Access will not be restricted to LDCs, but it has been informally agreed among the prospective contributors that a 'fair and substantial' share of supplementary credit should go to developing or non-industrialised members. This reflects the wish of OPEC contributors that the IMF should relieve them of a part of their recycling responsibilities and also the more general feeling that SFF resources may be too small to accommodate substantial borrowing (linked to quota size, as explained below) by two or three industrial countries.

Drawings on the SFF will be made under a standby arrangement lasting for between one and three years or under an extended fund facility arrangement over a three-year period.   SFF drawings will be linked to members' purchases in the credit tranches and will therefore be subject to the usual policy conditions, performance criteria and phasing by instalments. Under a standby arrangement supplementary finance of up to 12.5% of quota will be available to any member along with any unused portion of the first credit tranche and up to 30% of quota along with each of the upper credit tranches.   In special circumstances (undefined) of payments' disequilibrium purchases may be made by a member beyond the upper credit tranches (over 200% of quota) which will be wholly financed by supplementary credit.   Under an EFF arrangement a member's purchases will be financed from the IMF's ordinary and SFF resources in equal amounts with an overall limit of 140% of quota on each.

The cost of borrowing under the SFF will be equal to the rate of interest paid by the IMF to SFF contributors plus a margin of 0.2% per annum for the first three years of a purchase. Thereafter the margin will increase to 0.325% per annum. A subsidy account, similar to that in operation under the 1975 oil facility, designed to reduce the interest costs of LDC borrowers, was being considered by the IMF Executive Board in mid-1978.

The SFF clearly illustrates the constraints on the IMF. Its potential importance is great. In theory it will provide more adequate financing for countries prepared to undertake the necessary adjustment policies and could give confidence to private lenders during what will necessarily be a protracted period of adjustment. According to Solomon (1978), formerly adviser to the Board of Governors of the Federal Reserve System: 'The existence of such a facility and the role of the Fund in laying down policy conditions for countries to which it lends should encourage the private markets to continue the lending process'. Although the amount available is less than Witteveen's original target of SDR 14 billion, the facility is open-ended with scope for further contributions from participants and countries like the United Kingdom whose balance of payments and reserve position improve over the facility's life. It is also possible that the BIS will contribute but the details have not yet been worked out.

In practice, however, there are several drawbacks, not least the legislative delays in contributor countries which will prevent the SFF from operating before end-1978 at the earliest. The US Congress is particularly insistent on holding up ratification of the US contribution until it can attach a number of irrelevant clauses on human rights. More importantly the promised contributions are relatively small when set against the present and prospective international payments imbalance. In 1977 alone the aggregate current account deficit of LDCs was $25 billion and for advanced primary producers $13 billion and no significant improvement is expected in the next two or three years. Even with the SFF many countries' financing needs will, as now, greatly exceed what is available to them from the IMF; and the supplementary amounts may not be sufficient to induce more countries to use the Fund. Although SFF borrowing will be over a longer period than ordinary IMF credit, prospective borrowers may be deterred by the relatively high interest cost, the borrowing limits related to quotas and the fact that supplementary finance will largely be tied to use of the higher credit tranches complete with binding conditions. As now, borrowing from the IMF could remain a last resort measure.

The promised contributions to the SFF are also well below what contributors can afford. The OPEC countries have undertaken to provide only about one-seventh of their aggregate 1977 surplus, and the support of industrial countries was held back by their insistence on stringent conditions for SFF lending and that OPEC should find at least fifty per cent of the SFF's funds. Some of the smaller industrial countries such as the Netherlands were reluctant to contribute because they resented being excluded from the main decisions on the form of the new facility. These differences augur badly for the plans to top up the SFF which will be essential if payments' needs are to be met through this facility over the two to three year period until the next quota review takes effect. The present commitments of only SDR 8.75 billion may throw doubt on the IMF's ability to sustain a higher level of financing for very long, which could make banks less confident about renewing balance of payments loans and undermine the intended stabilising effect of the SFF on the international monetary system.

(b) IMF quotas

Probably the most effective and lasting way of enlarging IMF resources is through an increase in members' quotas (subscriptions). As outlined in Chapter One, general quota reviews have been held on six occasions since 1945 and substantial overall increases took place in 1959-60 (+50%), 1965-66 (+25%), 1969-70 (+25% together with special increases of SDR 5 billion for selected members) and 1975-78 (+32.5%). The last increase, agreed under the Sixth General Review, was ratified by members in March 1978, since when the theoretical size of the Fund's ordinary resources has been SDR 39 billion. In addition to the 32.5% general increase in quotas the Sixth Review also took into account certain group interests, a reflection of the changing political pressures within the Fund. The share of major oil producers was doubled to just under 10% and the collective share of LDCs was kept at its previous level of 29%. Within this framework the increases for individual countries and the way in which they would be paid to the Fund (in SDRs, other members' currencies or the member's own currency) were decided only after considerable bargaining.

However, the increase under the Sixth General Review is unlikely to be of more than temporary benefit to Fund liquidity. The increase in usable resources should be in the region of SDR 6-7 billion which would result in an immediate improvement in the ratio of IMF usable assets to liabilities from 40% at end-1977 to some 70% in 1978. But the enlarged quotas will involve greater access for members to the credit tranches which might be more widely used, particularly the less conditional first credit tranche, as oil facility drawings are repaid from 1978 onwards. Members will also be entitled to draw more from the IMF under the various special facilities such as the compensatory finance facility. In addition drawings under the new supplementary financing facility, although financed by separate IMF borrowing, will entail corresponding use of the credit tranches which may lead to an expansion in outstanding IMF credit.

It seems very likely, therefore, that members will take advantage of their new quota limits, particularly given the almost certain persistence of large-scale payments' imbalances in the short to medium term. Even a modest increase (allowing for repurchases) of about 20% in IMF lending in 1978-79 would put Fund liquidity under renewed strain (see Table 7.2) by 1980 at a time when some IMF creditor countries have begun to doubt the extent to which the IMF should rely on SFF-type borrowing operations.

Moreover, even allowing for the effects of the Sixth Review, IMF quotas have fallen sharply in relation to members' needs over the past decade. Quotas have declined as a proportion of members' international reserves from 30% in 1970 to 16% in 1977, as shown in Table 7.2. The ratio of IMF quotas to members' imports has also dropped from over 10% in 1966 to 4% in 1976-77, as can be seen in Table 7.3.

The quotas/imports ratio was 10.7% after the Fourth General Review in 1966, 9.6% after the Fifth Review in 1970, but only an estimated 4.3% after the implementation of the Sixth Review in mid-1978. This ratio may understate the declining value of IMF quotas since imports here exclude non-visible flows which have risen substantially in recent years.

In short, a substantial increase under the Seventh General Review,

Table 7.2   IMF quotas as a percentage of official reserves

Year	World	Industrial countries	Other developed	Oil exporters	Non-oil LDCs
1966	28	25	28	24	49
1970	30	28	28	29	45
1971	23	21	21	19	45
1972	20	19	13	15	33
1973	19	19	14	13	26
1974	16	19	16	4	25
1975	15	18	18	3	26
1976	14	16	18	3	20
1977 [1]	16	19	21	7	23

Source: *International Financial Statistics*

[1] Estimate for reserves

Table 7.3   IMF quotas as a percentage of imports

Year	World	Industrial countries	Other developed	Oil exporters	Non-oil LDCs
1966	11	10	9	11	13
1970	10	9	8	14	13
1971	9	8	9	12	14
1972	8	7	8	11	12
1973	7	6	7	9	10
1974	5	4	4	5	6
1975	4	4	4	3	6
1976	4	3	4	3	6
1977 [1]	4	-	-	-	-

Source: *International Financial Statistics*

[1] Estimate for imports

which was originally scheduled for agreement by February 1978, seems essential if the Fund is not to be circumscribed by liquidity constraints and is to be able to underpin commercial bank financing more effectively. A return to the 1970 quotas/international reserves ratio of 30% would imply a general quota increase of approximately 85% to a total of some SDR 70 billion.   A return to the 1970 quotas/imports ratio of 10% would mean a doubling of IMF quotas to SDR 80 billion in 1978.

As at previous reviews there have been wide differences of opinion among members.   The LDCs, not surprisingly, favour a 100% increase

but the major creditor nations have adopted their traditionally intransi-
gent position and were originally willing to concede only a minor 25-50%
increase, not with any economic justification but more as a minimum
acceptable political gesture.   Some creditors such as West Germany have
argued that a large increase is unnecessary in view of the substantial
amounts undrawn in the higher credit tranches, the wider access to IMF
credit now available under various special facilities and the anticipated
establishment of the SFF.   They have also stressed the vast expansion
since 1972-73 in new forms of payments' financing.

        These arguments are not very convincing.   IMF special facilities
have been temporary, like the oil facility, or have cut into resources
available for members in general, such as the 1976 expansion of the compensatory finance facility.   Access to other forms of finance is not always
open to MSA countries with large credit needs.   In other cases official
non-IMF borrowing is often short term and in short supply, while borrowing
from commercial banks has enabled countries to delay adjustment with
potentially serious implications.

        Final agreement had not been reached in mid-1978 but the most
likely outcome was a compromise general increase of 40-50%.   At best this
would mean an increase in usable resources of about SDR 10 billion (i.e.
that part of the increase paid to the IMF in SDRs or the usable currencies
of creditor countries) which would not be effective until 1980 at the
earliest.   It is extremely unlikely that this amount would have any more
permanent impact on the Fund's ability to react flexibly and on an adequate
scale to members' future credit demands than that agreed under the Sixth
Review.   A compromise increase of this nature would do little to bolster
the confidence of private creditors whose continued involvement in country
lending depends to some extent on the security which a more active IMF can
provide.

        The question is further complicated by the problem of selective
quota increases (over and above the general increase) for a few countries.
In theory these special increases are one way of strengthening Fund
liquidity, but in practice the scope for manoeuvre is limited.   The LDCs
have, predictably, made loud claims for a 'fairer' distribution of conditional liquidity without, of course, any intention of assuming greater
lending responsibilities within the IMF.   However, the industrial countries would oppose a further reduction of their collective share of quotas
(and consequently voting power) which has fallen from 73% in 1959 to 59%
in 1978.   They would also be reluctant to accept a permanent increase in
the voting power of OPEC countries from the present 10% to nearer 15% which
would give them a veto on major decisions.   There is probably room for
limited special increases for countries such as West Germany and Saudi
Arabia at the expense of China or possibly the United Kingdom, whose number
two position in the IMF has long been anomalous.   The wrangling and the
delays have hardly enhanced the IMF's authority in the international system.

(c) The general arrangements to borrow

        As outlined in Chapter Two the GAB has in the past proved a useful
backstop to Fund lending.   However, certain strains were evident
after the United Kingdom (SDR 3,360 million) and Italian (SDR 450 million)
applications for IMF credit in December 1976.   The Fund's straitened
liquidity position meant that G.10 countries were asked to provide a total
of SDR 2,900 million and Switzerland SDR 338 million.   Although the

United Kingdom no longer needs to draw — and started to make advance repayments in 1978 — the arrangements are now less reliable as a line of Fund defence in view of the continued payments weakness of several G.10 countries, notably the United States, France, Canada and Sweden.

On arithmetical as well as practical grounds there is a strong case for a major adjustment of GAB commitments if they are to have the same role as in 1962, let alone permit an expansion in IMF financing. The commitments have remained virtually unchanged while other economic variables have risen markedly. Only an unprecedented voluntary increase in the Japanese commitment to SDR 1 billion (yen 340 billion) at end-1976 restored the nominal total to just above the 1962 level from which it had fallen as a result of currency fluctuations. The original 1962 commitments represented 40% of IMF quotas and 60% of G.10 members' quotas, but by 1978 commitments had declined to the equivalent of only 17% of total Fund quotas. In 1962 SDR 6 billion was considered adequate to underpin G.10 countries' IMF drawing rights of SDR 12 billion. At end-1977, however, the latter, excluding super gold tranche positions, totalled over SDR 27 billion, making the relative size of the GAB less than half that originally negotiated.

These comparisons suggest that the GAB should be increased to at least SDR 10-15 billion. But the distribution of such an increase might be controversial because the 1962 individual country shares were arbitrary (see Chapter Two) and are now inappropriate. An increase on the basis of individual quota increases since 1962 would leave several countries with unsatisfactory shares, particularly Japan (too low) and Italy and the United Kingdom (too high). Alternatively, participants could commit the equivalent percentage of their international reserves, country by country (as in 1962) or the same average percentage of reserves as put up by participants in 1962. Here again it would be necessary to adjust some countries' disproportionate shares, notably the United States (too low) and the United Kingdom (too high). A third way might be to raise commitments by the percentage growth in individual countries' real GDP since 1962 or decide on an overall total of, say, SDR 12 billion and base individual increases on the latest available GDP data. A final possibility would be to restore the value of 1962 commitments by weak industrial countries within a predetermined total and allocate the balance in proportion to G.10 contributions to the January 1977 BIS safety net for sterling.

Other reforms would be even more controversial, not least enlarged membership. According to Morgan Guaranty (January 1977) the GAB is outmoded in its present form because it excludes several of the world's largest surplus countries such as OPEC members. However, the inclusion of Saudi Arabia and Iran might have drawbacks. It would not necessarily, judging by these two countries' less than generous contributions to the oil facility, lead to a substantial increase in GAB resources, particularly given the relatively low annual interest rate (4-6%) on loans by participants. It might lead to pressure from Australia and some smaller European countries to become participants, which could disrupt what is now a useful forum for co-ordinating, or trying to co-ordinate, G.10 adjustment strategies. Enlarged membership could become necessary if the scope of GAB lending were extended to cover not just G.10 borrowing from the IMF but other countries' drawings as well. It might then be possible for GAB financing to take the form of block loans to the IMF to cover several, fairly small, prospective drawings but this is a remote contingency at present.

An increase in GAB resources to SDR 10-15 billion from the present participants would give the IMF greater operational flexibility and allow it to retain its influence over potential industrial country borrowers. Yet the chances of reform are slight before the next formal renewal of the arrangements in 1980 and even then few participants may be willing to take on more onerous financial burdens in an uncertain economic climate. For the future the 'spirit of broad and willing co-operation' mentioned in the 1962 agreement seems conspicuously lacking.

(d) The SDR

The SDR has fulfilled few of its advocates' original hopes and in 1978 formed an insignificant proportion (4%) of world reserves. The reform exercise failed to enhance the SDR's status, and Witteveen's proposal for an SDR-dollar substitution account, as set out in Chapter Six, had not been accepted by all the major countries in mid-1978.

One remedy, which would also enlarge the IMF's financing role, would be a new allocation of SDRs — independent of any substitution scheme — to follow the first and only allocation of 1970-72. An allocation in 1979-80 would have several advantages, including that of keeping the SDR facility viable. It might alleviate, under IMF supervision, the payments problems of deficit countries, particularly the LDCs and minor OECD countries whose need for reserves has not been substantially reduced by the adoption of floating exchange rates in the major economies. Many LDCs are pegged to a major currency and have experienced wide fluctuations in their payments positions since 1973 as a result of movements in the 'peg'. An SDR allocation could help to offset the recent instability in primary producers' (not just LDCs) export earnings and to maintain the confidence of commercial lenders in the medium-term prospects of likely 'problem' countries.

An SDR allocation might also lead to a more satisfactory composition of countries' reserves. There is no conclusive evidence but it seems likely that some recipients would use their SDR allocations to repay outstanding commercial bank loans. This in turn would result in improved debt-service ratios and greater freedom to employ future export earnings in productive development. The amount of such an allocation might be controversial, but a figure of SDR 5-8 billion seems reasonable from the viewpoint of debtor and creditor countries. On the one hand it would fill the gap caused by the shortfall in SFF contributions mentioned above and on the other it would not interfere with adjustment measures now under way or exacerbate world inflation.

Not surprisingly an allocation is strongly favoured by LDCs possibly skewed in their favour (the SDR/aid link). However, most developed countries are opposed to anything other than a symbolic allocation to rescue the SDR facility from premature demise. In contrast to the late 1960s there is no clear-cut 'global need' for an allocation as prescribed in the IMF Articles and no other justification was included in the Amended Articles. The measurement of reserve needs is complicated by the uncertainty surrounding the future role of monetary gold and floating exchange rates and by the increased availability of private credit since 1970. Some creditors would regard an increase in unconditional liquidity (SDRs) as inappropriate in view of the perceived adjustment needs; and others like West Germany simply feel that there is already an over-abundance of international liquidity. According to the 1975 Annual Report of the Bundesbank, the 'great elasticity' in world reserves 'detracts from balance of payments discipline'.

Less conservative developed countries led by Belgium have advocated further improvements in the SDR's characteristics before a new allocation takes place. As outlined in Chapter Three the method of valuation was amended in March 1978 and further proposals, including a higher interest rate and the abolition of the reconstitution (repayment) provisions, have been considered in the IMF Executive Board and the Interim Committee in the first part of 1978. Even if the proposed reforms are accepted, the fundamental differences of opinion on the SDR's role will remain. The present impasse between debtors and creditors could prevent a new allocation, at least until the start of the next basic period in 1981, and while it continues there is no chance of introducing an SDR/aid link on the lines suggested in Chapter Three. The continuing opposition of the United States and West Germany, which hold an effective veto, seems likely to condemn the link indefinitely to 'reference for further consideration'.

Medium-term prospects

Realistically, therefore, the prospects for major changes are not encouraging. As Table 7.4 shows, the resources available to the IMF in the period 1978-81 are unlikely to exceed SDR 40 billion.

Table 7.4   Usable IMF resources 1978-81

SDR billion

	Minimum	Maximum
Usable currencies and SDRs, end-October 1977	7.2	7.2
Net increase in usable currencies 1978-81	+3.5	+5.5
(assuming that 12-15 of the 24 members which were not Fund debtors at end-1977, but were not in the currency budget, make their currencies usable in this period)		
Gold sales (Chapter Six, p.67)	+2.0	+2.0
Sixth quota review	+6.0	+7.0
(involving inflows of SDR 6 billion — out of the SDR 10 billion total increase — in presently usable currencies plus a possible SDR 1 billion of the remaining SDR 4 billion which could be paid in SDRs)		
Seventh quota review	+9.0	+11.5
(on the assumption that quotas will increase equiproportionately by 50% or SDR 19.5 billion with SDR 9 billion of this in quotas of members whose currencies are presently usable and a maximum 25% of the balance being paid in SDRs)		
Supplementary credit facility (1978-1981)	+8.8	+10.0
Total	36.5	43.2

The total available seems inadequate when compared with the OECD forecast (December 1977) of a $30 billion current account deficit for LDCs

in 1978 alone. Assuming little change in the magnitude and distribution
of the glcbal payments imbalance in the period to 1982, the financing
needs of many countries will continue to exceed what the IMF can provide.
Even in the few cases where countries have sufficient IMF resources to
cover a given deficit, they are unlikely to draw the full amount if their
payments problems are deep-rooted or persistent.   The obstacles, institutional and political, to the expansion of the Fund make it necessary to
consider more radical operational changes which are examined in the
following chapter.

CHAPTER EIGHT

THE IMF AND ALTERNATIVE FINANCING MECHANISMS

Even on the most optimistic assumptions the scope of IMF influence
will be restricted in the medium term unless new proposals are tried. This
chapter examines two possibilities — the establishment of a new financing
institution to assist the IMF; and closer links between the IMF and the
commercial banks.

A new IMF-IBRD institution

One possible way of dealing with the prospective gap in official
financing over the medium term would be to establish a new institution
involving both the IMF and the IBRD.   The new corporation could be financed by bond issues on the international capital markets and would therefore require little equity capital.   The corporation's bond issues would
be bought not by all members of the IMF and IBRD but by surplus countries,
OPEC and industrial, able and willing to lend.   Such a corporation would
almost certainly command a first-class rating in the market because its
liabilities would be backed by the guarantee of subscribers and its assets
would take the form of claims on the IMF and IBRD, as explained below.
Apart from bond finance, the corporation might also take over and administer the resources of the IMF trust fund, which is at present managed
separately from other IMF facilities with the IMF as trustee.

The new corporation's funds would be available for two types of
lending, either to the IBRD and IDA for programme loans (outlined in
Chapter Seven) or to the IMF for loans on normal credit tranche criteria.
An important feature would be that the corporation's lending would be
integrated into a coherent programme for individual countries, which took
account of medium-term payments problems and longer-term development
strategy.   Such lending could involve discrete pressure, through the IMF
in particular, to ensure that prospective country recipients were following
appropriate adjustment policies.   It might also be used to improve countries' debt-service profiles, especially with regard to outstanding
commercial loans, and this could lead to close links between the corporation
and the international banks.

The corporation could be run by a Washington-based governing board
on which subscribers would be represented.   Voting power on the board
would correspond to the amount subscribed, a feature which might attract
the major oil producers whose influence in the IMF and IBRD is currently
restricted.   The board would be responsible for deciding whether or not
to lend and, once the decision had been taken, whether to lend to the IMF
or the IBRD.   In practice it would have a quasi-supervisory role which

would not detract greatly from the authority of the existing IMF and IBRD
Executive Boards.   The new board could be advised by a small staff of not
more than twenty or thirty whose main function would be to prepare the
necessary analyses and background information.

Such an institution might offer a way round the difficulties —
examined in Chapter Seven — of raising finance through increases in IMF
quotas and IBRD capital.   It might facilitate smoother recycling, assuming that the incentives were sufficient for OPEC participation, and by
encouraging IMF-IBRD co-operation would help to clarify the currently
blurred distinction between balance of payments adjustment and development
aid.   At the very least the requirements of deficit countries would become more apparent and there would be some benefit to world trade.
Although the corporation would not bail out the banks its effective operation could increase the chances of earlier repayments on commercial loans.
More generally it would strengthen the international financial system while
protracted adjustment processes, both to higher oil prices and among country groups, work their way through the economic and political systems of
IMF and IBRD members.

In practical terms, however, the chance of such an institution
being established in the near term is small.   Even if it were agreed in
principle there would be technical and procedural delays and the proposed
IMF supplementary financing facility has to a large extent pre-empted the
resources and political will for a radical alternative.   Nevertheless the
SFF has been awkwardly grafted on to the IMF's institutional framework,
with its attendant political controversies, and there are doubts also on
the extent to which the IMF can borrow in this manner in the future.   If,
as is possible, SFF funds prove inadequate, a corporation on the lines
suggested might become a more viable proposition after 1980-81.

The IMF and the commercial banks

A second important way for the IMF to extend its influence and
expand the resources effectively available to it is through closer co-operation with the commercial banks.   As explained in Chapter Five, the banks
have increasingly come to rely on an IMF standby as a country's passport
to commercial credit, and parallel lending, as it is known, has a vital
role to play in the next few years.   So far, however, there is no co-
ordinated approach to this kind of lending and no systematic exchanges of
information.   All that exist at present are informal IMF contacts with
the top US banks: the major banks outside the United States and the smaller
US banks have few links with the IMF and no means of developing a closer
relationship.   The large US banks invariably place far greater weight on
their own explicit judgements than on the implicit and necessarily guarded
views of the IMF staff.

Closer collaboration was considered, inconclusively, by the IMF
Executive Board in 1977.   There are a number of difficulties, not least
because the outlook and interests of the Fund and the banks differ markedly,
as they do between IMF members and between banks according to their size
and country of origin.   The IMF is an international institution, responsible to its member governments and designed to provide conditional, medium-
term adjustment finance.   Commercial banks on the other hand are profit-
oriented concerns which are responsible to depositors, shareholders and
domestic regulators.   Their international operations cover self-liquidating

trade credit, project loans and finance for foreign companies and financial institutions as well as balance of payments lending to governments.

It is therefore easier to say what forms of co-operation are neither practical nor desirable. For instance, legal or contractual links have been widely canvassed and in mid-1977 Hauge of Manufacturers Hanover Trust proposed the formation of a joint IMF-bank committee to examine the possibilities, but so far nothing has come of this proposal. It is difficult to see how formal links would benefit either party. Apart from technical problems, they might entail a loss of flexibility and blur responsibility in areas such as debt rescheduling negotiations. They could involve banks in unnecessary, restrictive commitments with regard to their lending criteria and the overall composition of their loan portfolios. They could also become a channel for official pressures which could be against the banks' longer-term interests. On the other side, formal links could undermine the IMF's supra-national role if LDCs felt that the Fund was siding with the banks against country borrowers.

An equally unsatisfactory proposal made by Ponto of Dresdner Bank, reported in *Euromoney* (May 1977), was for the IMF to provide credit ratings for individual countries. The Fund is not equipped to act as a large-scale Moodys and, if it did, would risk being held responsible for commercial loan failures or being drawn into spheres of lending which were not its own. Some banks might feel obliged to accept IMF credit assessments, to the detriment of their existing relationships with borrower governments, and the confidence of deficit members in the IMF would also suffer. Governments might be less forthcoming in consultations, which would damage the quality of IMF reports and of IMF influence in general.

As a third approach Burns and Wallich of the US Federal Reserve Board proposed, in 1977, an international 'rule of law' with much wider supervisory powers for the IMF over commercial bank lending. Thus, according to Burns, the IMF should undertake surveillance of private credit flows to the extent that an 'IMF certificate of good standing' became essential before a country could borrow on the markets. Similarly, Wallich advocated a more direct disciplinary role for the Fund in commercial loan negotiations, whereby banks would inform the IMF and their own central banks of prospective international loans. In cases of doubt, banks would not lend without IMF blessing. In the words of *Euromoney*, this would 'get the banks off the hook' and they would 'be banks again, rather than credit agencies'.

In practice this kind of IMF surveillance could lead to considerable problems. To many commercial bankers warnings of chaos, unless the IMF can rapidly impose some order, risk provoking the crises they seek to avoid. Moreover, few banks actually wish to cut back on their total international lending and few see a need for a general IMF rescue operation — indeed the major banks would certainly resent IMF 'interference'. Private flows of finance could be seriously disrupted if IMF approval of borrowers' policies or of particular loans were a pre-condition of bank credit. Some IMF members, particularly LDC borrowers, would see Fund supervision as further evidence of the insensitivity of industrial countries and international institutions to their needs.

Informal less ambitious forms of co-operation are therefore more likely to be successful. The two most realistic avenues are more systematic exchanges of information and parallel lending.

A start has been made in this sphere with the preparation, by the Bank for International Settlements, of a booklet for the guidance of commercial banks. The booklet will list the available sources of economic information on individual countries and will also contain a checklist of questions which central banks in industrial countries can recommend banks to ask country loan applicants. Although the questionnaire will not be mandatory on banks and will only cover basic data such as GNP, inflation, balance of payments and external debt (already required by major banks), it could help to guide the less experienced lenders and provide a justification for refusing particular loans. The IMF can assist in this process, through its consultations, by promoting these informal guidelines and encouraging greater openness in borrowing countries.

There is also a strong case for wider circulation of IMF documents. This could be done through central banks to whom IMF reports are routinely transmitted. It would not be difficult to establish a consultative process in which private lenders could discuss IMF information with their central banks, but without the latter advising whether or on what scale loans should be made to a particular country. (Even more than the IMF, central banks cannot, for political reasons, be seen to act as arbiters of sovereign risk or accept responsibility for banks' credit assessments.) Such consultations would contribute to a better climate of information in which central banks could be a channel of communication between commercial banks and the IMF and smooth the inevitable changes in working practice on both sides.

If the principle of wider dissemination of information were accepted, the contents of the reports to be circulated would have to be agreed among IMF members. In practice the Fund would probably be authorised to circulate only the background economic data from its annual country reports or more compact statistical summaries. Administrative resources permitting, this information could include all available details on external debt and could be updated more frequently than at present to cover performance under standbys, which often involve quarterly monitoring of data. On the other hand circulation of staff appraisals of members' policies would be unacceptable for several reasons, not least the adverse effect this could have on their quality and frankness. It could also lead to conflicts of judgement between the IMF and the banks, to no-one's benefit.

Initially perhaps the IMF background reports would have a fairly narrow circulation. They might be restricted to banks with loan applications from IMF members. In the case of syndicated bank loans the lead banks could be allowed to pass Fund documents to prospective participants. Once the system had been developed, circulation could be extended to other 'interested' banks.

Under this type of system the IMF could provide information by consent. It would not direct bank lending in any way nor impede private judgement; and the responsibilities of the two parties would remain distinct. The main barrier is the opposition of LDCs to even limited disclosures which they see as a breach of confidence by the IMF and a form of collusion to force deficit countries into the more conditional higher credit tranches. The countries willing to accept the idea already publish comprehensive economic and financial data. Progress here, as in other areas, is likely to be slow and piecemeal.

Since 1976 the major banks have increasingly recognised the interest they share with the IMF in adjustment.   In several cases, listed in Chapter Five, further bank lending has been made dependent on the borrower adopting an economic programme approved under an IMF standby.

The advantages of this strategy are clear-cut.   According to Taylor (1977): 'The IMF's access to information, the analytical skill of its staff and its ability to enforce strict loan conditions, combined with the financial resources of the private banking system creates a mutually beneficial opportunity'.   Closer IMF involvement gives the banks some assurance, previously lacking, that borrowers will pursue appropriate policies without making demands on the banks directly.   Extension of parallel lending would imply a greater use of official facilities, but it would have the advantage that banks might feel able to lend more than they otherwise would.   In the longer term it would lay the basis for a continuing important role for the banks in balance of payments lending irrespective of temporary shifts in market confidence.

From the IMF's point of view arrangements of this sort can 'gear up' the amount of finance effectively attached to the ordinary credit tranches.   The much greater resources available can help prospective borrowers to overcome their natural political reluctance to accept IMF conditions, without there being any relaxation in the Fund's policy standards.   A good example of this was the United Kingdom's $1.5 billion loan from the euromarkets in February 1977 which supplemented its agreed IMF drawing.   The same could happen in the cases of Turkey, Portugal, Zambia and other countries which negotiated standby programmes with the IMF in 1977 and 1978.

The success of these arrangements depends on a three way co-operation between national governments, commercial banks and the IMF. Governments must be prepared to deal simultaneously with the IMF and with the banks, while the latter must resist the temptation to allow their potentially lucrative loans to be a substitute for adjustment.   So far the initiative for parallel financing has come from the banks and there is scope for more active IMF involvement.   The IMF need not merely provide conditional finance.   If a standby applicant so requested, the staff might possibly take steps to discover what bank finance would be available after the standby had been agreed — a form of prior gearing.   The IMF would be in a position to inform banks of the probable terms of the standby and give supplementary background data, again subject to the approval of the country involved.   The problem of confidentiality would be lessened if this information were circulated only to the banks which had declared an active interest in a particular loan.

If this were to happen — and Turkey allowed the IMF to circulate confidential data among potential bank lenders during its negotiations with the Fund in early 1978 — the IMF would in no way control bank lending. The banks would be free to ignore IMF overtures and continue as now if they wished; and borrowing countries would not be forced to do anything against their will.   The IMF could, however, act decisively as a catalyst in improving members' adjustment and financing prospects.

Co-financing

The extension of co-financing (joint lending by the IBRD or

egional development banks and commercial banks) is an encouraging precedent for parallel lending. It is also one way of easing LDC pressures on
the IMF to expand its aid-related operations. Between the fourth quarter
of 1975 and the fourth quarter of 1977 five such arrangements were agreed,
three by the IBRD and two by the Inter-American Development Bank (IADB),
and several more have since been negotiated. The two institutions have
developed sophisticated methods which could be adapted by other international agencies. In both cases private banks make separate but comp-
lementary loans which are disbursed under normal market conditions independent of IBRD or IADB credit. The IBRD and IADB provide the technical
appraisals of projects, assist in the negotiations between country borrowers and commercial banks and sometimes act as collecting agents for the
banks.

The IBRD formula involves two distinct contracts, between the
borrower and the IBRD on the one hand and between the borrower and the
commercial banks on the other. The banks are given the support of an
optional cross-default clause which authorises the IBRD to suspend disbursements or accelerate repayments on its loan should the borrower
default on the commercial bank loan. The borrower is required to channel
payment of fees, interest and principal on the commercial loan through a
special account in the name of the IBRD at the commercial bank. There
is provision also for the IBRD to monitor the use of the commercial loan
and to pass on all relevant information.

The IADB relies on a single loan contract between the borrower and
the IADB. Under this arrangement the commercial banks buy participations
in the IADB loan, the balance of which is funded from the IADB's own
resources. The default clauses are very narrow and, until recently, the
banks' interests were protected solely by the good offices of the IADB.
These arrangements have worked well in the past but have had to be revised
in 1978 as more of the major banks, accustomed to considerable independence
in loan negotiations, have entered the field. In two cases, involving
projects in Panama and Argentina, the banks have incorporated new provisions including the right to be consulted if the borrower defaults or otherwise misbehaves.

Co-financing has benefited borrowers, commercial banks and international institutions. It is convenient, relatively cheap and suitable
for projects which might otherwise be neglected given a possible slowdown
in commercial lending. It offers banks greater protection at little cost,
estimated by Derecho (1976) as '$\frac{1}{8}$% off the interest rate or one year on the
tenor of a normal medium-term Euro-credit'. Few, if any, LDCs would
jeopardise their access to concessional finance by defaulting on IBRD or
IADB related loans.

For international institutions co-financing, like parallel financing, can gear up official loans without any relaxation of standards. It
is particularly valuable where development needs exceed the financial
capacity of one commercial syndicate or one multilateral body. In addition
the international organisations do not have to assume significantly greater
responsibilities: in the event of a default on a commercial loan they would
probably be obliged to step in anyway, co-financing agreement or not. There
are thus several practicable ways of extending IMF influence which could be
explored without infringing members' sovereignty or impeding commercial bank
international operations. Nevertheless, the conflicting interests of
deficit and surplus countries and the dangers of appearing to be partisan
could well restrict IMF initiatives in this area in the near term.

Conclusion

In sum, therefore, the need for countries to place greater emphasis on adjustment has become increasingly apparent in recent years. The dangers of not doing so are clearly illustrated by the economic problems of the United Kingdom in late 1976 and of Turkey in early 1978. The need for the IMF to play a more central role in the adjustment process has also been increasingly recognised by national governments, bank supervisory authorities and commercial banks. Through conditional financial support and surveillance of economic policies, the IMF has had a special responsibility in helping countries like Mexico in 1976-77 to restore payments equilibrium.

The basis for extending the IMF's influence already exists in the power to impose conditions on its lending, in the recent moves to expand its resources (such as the supplementary financing facility) and in the broad powers to monitor members' exchange rate policies which could eventually lead to an agreed code of practice governing intervention and target zones. Another hopeful sign is the growing practice among commercial banks of linking their loans informally to IMF standby agreements, a practice which could be considerably extended and modified to the benefit of banks, the IMF and international adjustment in general.

However, the necessary changes are bound to take time in view of the deep political division among members over the appropriate nature of IMF operations. Indeed, the conservative views of important creditors like West Germany could well limit IMF financing initiatives to a level below that necessary to cover prospective medium-term needs. At the same time IMF surveillance powers are not clearly defined in the Amended Articles and are crucially dependent on co-operation by national governments which has often been tentative since 1972. Although the IMF's achievements in the past have been considerable, it seems unlikely at present that individual governments will have the vision to allow the IMF to fulfil its potential. If it does not, the consequences for international adjustment — in the form of protectionist policies, instability of exchange rates and wider imbalances — could be serious over the medium term.

REFERENCES AND SELECT BIBLIOGRAPHY

IMF publications

International Monetary Reform: Documents of the Committee of Twenty, 1974

Reform of the International Monetary System: A Report by the Executive Directors, 1972

The Role of Exchange Rates in the Adjustment of International Payments: A Report by the Executive Directors, 1970

Selected Decisions, Seventh Issue, 1975

Summary Proceedings – Annual Meeting 1976: Supplement – Proposed Second Amendment, November 1976

Books and articles

Abdalla, I. S., 'Bringing democracy into the world monetary system', *Euromoney*, April 1977

Aschinger, F. E., 'The controversy surrounding international liquidity', *Euromoney*, February 1976

Aufricht, H., *The International Monetary Fund, Legal Bases, Structure, Functions*, Stevens 1963

Barrett, V., 'Monetary reform: the umpteenth round', *Euromoney*, February 1975

Bartlett, J., 'International liquidity – a re-examination', unpublished MS, University College of North Wales, Bangor, 1977

'Bifocals for Washington', *The Economist*, 24 September 1977

'BIS survey of commercial bank lending', *The Economist*, 15 June 1977

Boeker, P. H., 'The LDC debt problem', Testimony to the Sub-Committee of the House of Representatives Banking Committee, Washington, 5 April 1977

Brimmer, A. F., 'International banking attracts more funds for foreigners than it lends', *American Banker*, 5 April 1977

Burns, A. F., 'US bank lending to LDCs', Testimony to the US Senate Banking Committee (reported in *Financial Times*, 11 March 1977)

Burns, A. F., 'The need for order in international finance', Address to the Columbia University Graduate School of Business, New York, 12 April 1977

Carson, C. W., 'Remarks at the Financial Analysts Federation, Seventh Annual Banking Symposium, New York', *American Banker*, 10 March 1977

Cooper, R., 'Currency devaluation in developing countries', *Princeton University Essays in International Finance*, No. 86, June 1971

'Coping with the imbalance in international payments', *Morgan Guaranty Trust Company of New York - World Financial Markets*, January 1977

Costanzo, G. A., 'Lending to developing countries - why the gloom is overdone', *Euromoney*, May 1975

Crockett, A., *International Money*, Washington 1977

Dale, W. B., 'Address before the 63rd Session of the Economic and Social Council of the United Nations', 13 July 1977, *IMF Survey*, 18 July 1977

Derecho, S. D., 'Co-financing between international agencies and the private sector', *Euromoney*, March 1976

De Vries, R., 'The international debt situation', *Morgan Guaranty Trust Company of New York - World Financial Markets*, June 1977

'The EEC - a protectionist Christmas parcel', *The Economist*, 24 December 1977

'From free trade to adjustment', *The Economist*, 31 December 1977

Gold, J., *Voting and Decisions in the International Monetary Fund*, IMF, Washington, 1972

Gold, J., *Special Drawing Rights, Character and Use*, IMF Pamphlet Series No. 13, Washington, 1970 (Second Edition)

Goreux, L. M., 'Recovery of commodity prices expected to slow', *IMF Survey*, 3 March 1977

Halm, G., 'The IMF and the flexibility of exchange rates', *Princeton University Essays in International Finance*, No. 83, March 1971

'Heimman cracks down on international lending', *Financial Times*, 11 January 1978

'The IMF', *The Economist*, 4 March 1978

'IMF to the rescue', *Euromoney*, April 1977

'International credit markets', *Morgan Guaranty Trust Company of New York - World Financial Markets*, December 1977

'International lending by US banks', *Federal Reserve Bank of New York Quarterly Review*, August 1977

Islam, N., 'Jamaica and the developing countries, reflections on Jamaica', *Princeton University Essays in International Finance*, No. 115, April 1976

Johnson, H. G., 'World inflation and the international monetary system', *Three Banks Review*, September 1975

Kafka, A., 'The IMF: reform without reconstruction', *Princeton University Essays in International Finance*, No. 118, October 1976

Katz, S., 'Devaluation bias in the Bretton Woods system', *Banca Nazionale Del Lavoro Quarterly Review*, June 1972

Kirbyshire, J. A., 'Should developments in the euro-markets be a source of concern to regulatory authorities?', *Bank of England Quarterly Bulletin*, March 1977 (Talk to the *Financial Times* Euro-Markets Conference, London, 23 February 1977)

'The LDC debt problem', *Amex Bank Review*, Volume 4, No. 3, March 1977

Nash, J. M., 'Remarks at the Financial Analysts Federation Seventh Annual Banking Symposium, New York', *American Banker*, 10 March 1977

'The OPEC surplus', *Citibank Monthly Review*, July 1977

Polak, J. J., *Valuation and Rate of Interest on the SDR*, IMF Pamphlet Series No.18, Washington 1974

Richardson, G., 'Speech to the Association of Reserve City Bankers, Phoenix, Arizona, 4 April 1977', *Bank of England Quarterly Bulletin*, June 1977

Rockefeller, D., 'Problems, perspectives and responsibilities in international finance', *Chase Manhattan Monthly Review*, September 1976

Roosa, R. V., 'Some questions remaining, reflections on Jamaica', *Princeton University Essays in International Finance*, No. 115, April 1976

'The sick men of the euro-markets', *Euromoney*, March 1978

Solomon, Robert, 'The IMF and market borrowing', *The Banker*, March 1978

Stankard, F., 'Remarks at the Financial Analysts Federation, Seventh Annual Banking Symposium, New York', *American Banker*, 10 March 1977

Strodes, J., 'Governor Wallich wants the IMF to advise LDC lenders', *Euromoney*, April 1977

Taylor, H., 'Commercial banks and the IMF', *Euromoney*, May 1977

'Towards protection', *The Times*, 23 February 1978

Triffin, R., 'Triffin's view of the world monetary system', *Euromoney*, July 1975

'US clarifies rules for foreign loans', *The Times*, 9 January 1978

'The US economy', *The Times*, 20 February 1978

'The US trade deficit and policy alternatives', *Morgan Guaranty Trust Company of New York - World Financial Markets*, September 1977

Waldheim, K., 'Remarks to the 17th Ministerial Meeting of ECLA, Guatemala City, 2 May 1977', *Financial Times*, 3 May 1977

Wallich, H. C., 'Statement before the Sub-sommittee on Financial Institutions, Supervision, Regulation and Insurance of the Committee on Banking, Finance and Urban Affairs, of the US House of Representatives', 23 March 1977

Wallich, H. C., 'How much private bank lending is enough?', Talk to a symposium on developing countries' debt sponsored by the Export-Import Bank, Washington, 21 April 1977

'Where the buck stops', *The Economist*, 18 March 1978

Williamson, J., 'International liquidity - a survey', *Economic Journal*, September 1973

Williamson, J., 'The benefits and costs of an international monetary non-system, reflections on Jamaica', *Princeton University Essays in International Finance*, No. 115, April 1976

Williamson, J., *The Failure of World Monetary Reform*, Nelson, 1977

Witteveen, H. J., 'The emerging international monetary system', *IMF Survey*, 21 June 1976

Witteveen, H. J., 'World stabilisation policies', *IMF Survey*, 6 December 1976

Witteveen, H. J., 'The world economic situation', *IMF Survey*, 16 May 1977

Witteveen, H. J., 'The current economic situation in the industrial countries', *IMF Survey*, 1 August 1977

'World payments trends', *Morgan Guaranty Trust Company of New York - World Financial Markets*, April 1977

General sources

Official

Bank of England, *Quarterly Bulletin*
Bank for International Settlements, *Annual Reports*
Deutsche Bundesbank, *Annual Reports*
International Bank for Reconstruction and Development, *Annual Reports*
International Monetary Fund, *Annual Reports*
International Monetary Fund, *International Financial Statistics*, monthly
International Monetary Fund, *Press Releases*
International Monetary Fund, *IMF Survey*
Organisation for Economic Co-operation and Development, *Economic Outlook*, half-yearly
Organisation for Economic Co-operation and Development, *List of Bodies of the Organisation, Mandates, Membership, Officers* (Paris 1977)

Other

American Banker, daily
The Banker, monthly
Citibank Economic Review, monthly
The Economist, weekly
The Economist Financial Report, fortnightly
Euromoney, monthly
Federal Reserve Bank of New York Quarterly Review
Financial Times, daily
The Times, daily
World Financial Markets, Morgan Guaranty Trust Company, monthly